What people are saying about
Mark Yarnell and his books...

"All we have to do is pick up either a book or a tape that has Mark Yarnell's thoughts and ideas in them and we are once again... FIRED UP and ready to go the extra mile...He somehow manages to inspire us and stop us from making the mistake that most people in this industry have done...and that is...to quit. Mark Yarnell is definitely one of the greatest Network Marketers that has ever walked the face of this planet . I would recommend his materials and ideas to anyone who is serious about getting serious in this amazing business."

Edison Apolonio
Senior Executive - Independent Distributor
Neways International (Australia) Pty Ltd

"Mark Yarnell's concepts of Network Marketing have truly made an enormous impact on our business. We have been involved in Network Marketing for 10 years and are overjoyed to inform you that our newest and last venture along with your teachings has grossed us more in the last ten months than we had accomplished in the last ten years!"

Matt and Nanette Ream
Freedom Health

*"Mark Yarnell's words never fail to bring focus and clarity to my goals. He has the ability to just cut to the chase and eliminate the irrelevant minutia. And there is incredible power in that for us all. Bringing all our energy to bear on the essential things we want to achieve is exhilarating. This will be my best year yet.
Thanks, Mark!"*

Larry Loewenstein
National Marketing Director
Legacy For Life

"Mr. Mark Yarnell has had an extreme influence on my life. His experience and teachings on business ethics, strategies, and leadership have helped mold my thinking and have been passed on to many other inquiring, open-minded individuals. Thank you for having such a positive impact on my life and contributing to my success. I would recommend his thoughts and insights to anyone in the field of business or marketing."

Ryan Blackport
"The Free Network"

"Thank you, MarkYarnell, for your teachings, insights and education on the value and professionalism of network marketing. Thanks in large part to your work, I have gone from being the biggest skeptic on MLM to being on track for a $50k month income. You have given people like me the information that allows us to understand the legitimacy and necessary ingredients to be successful in MLM.

Thanks, Thanks, Thanks!"

Greg Lawlor
Excel Communications

"It is an understatement to try and limit his contributions to network marketing alone, for Mark has deeply inspired me in ways far beyond that field. His deep thoughts, which he freely shares with the whole world often have the high wisdom of spiritualism, but without the narrow confinements of religion.

As a student of the natural laws, I know that MarkYarnell has made life itself his own teacher, and this earthlife, a school. May God continue to expand his wisdom, giving him better clarity, so that the problems he may encounter today will always lead him to great discoveries of tomorrow in this ever expanding universe of ours."

Barrister Ike Unegbe
Lawyer/Investment Consultant
Nigeria

"Mark Yarnell's contributions are the most groundbreaking ideas we have come across in the Network Marketing industry. Mark's refreshingly honest approach is both brave and insightful. His words are a mentor to us, a constant source of inspiration."

Matthew Earl & Suzanne Lozano
Kleeneze Europe PLC

"Read this book! After stumbling around in network marketing for 6 years, I decided to listen to what Mark Yarnell had to say. What Mark has to say works! I now earn a significant, full time income in network marketing. Thanks, Mark Yarnell."

Rich Morgan
Legacy For Life

"I would like to personally thank Mark Yarnell for sharing his great experiences with me."

Daniel Aw
Singapore
SUCCESSTOGETHER

"Since attending Mark Yarnell's seminar, my business has increased significantly and the foundation has substance and depth. I easily identify with his work ethics and know that as my team uses his management concepts the heights that we will reach in the near future will be amazing. Thanks for being there for us."

Hank Heister
Integris Global

"Over the last 15 months or so, I have been reading Mark Yarnell's concepts and have benefited in large part from his insights. He has shared from his experience and heart in a straightforward manner, eliminating all the hype which creeps into so many MLM writings. Keep the encouragement and helpful ideas coming! Wishing you the best."

Don Burnett
Nikken Platinum Health Consultant

"I wonder if you have any idea of the depth of the impact of your teachings with those of us who are in an older age group than you yourself. We all know of the benefits from being "coachable," but that's easier to say and harder to do for the "old dogs." But I've been super impressed with your ability to "lay it on the line" in a very understandable way...over and over again. And I appreciate that. I am thankful to you every day that I begin again with another new person in my business."

Stan Holmes
ED/NTD Excel Communications, Inc.

"Mark Yarnell's simple, easy to understand, "even-a-three-year-old-can-understand-it" style helps me make sense of this sometimes crazy business we call MLM. I live and breathe by your assertion that "success is in the numbers" and I teach it to my downline. It was a dream come true when I saw you speak at a recent Jafra Cosmetics conference. Most of my downline know that I quote you all the time."

Arleatha "Lisa" Washington
Jafra Cosmetics, District Manager

"Fifteen years ago, Mark Yarnell taught me how to build a large network marketing organization. I refused to listen. He earned millions. I failed. A few years later, I finally came to my senses and decided to follow his advice . It was a great decision. I'm now earning more than most corporate executives -- and I don't have to get up and go to work every morning. Mark has a very simple formula that can get you out of traffic, off Maalox , and out of 60-hour weeks. This book is your ticket out of the stress of Corporate America."

Lynn Beene
National Marketing Director
Legacy for Life

"I am a District Manager II with Jafra Cosmetics and have really benefited from the timely advise in your book (Your First Year in Network Marketing), and the weekly thought has been RIGHT ON THE MONEY! I have built my business on some of the same person-to-person efforts you encourage. In addition, I have watched a family member attempt to build in all the wrong ways. After reading your book, I encouraged him to GO GET ONE and read it also so he could stop spinning his wheels and wasting his money! These are my favorite pieces of advice - 1. Don't baby-sit whiners! 2. Invest your time and $ in real people - not internet or phone "leads". 3. Sponsor a strong front line and don't do the work for them. All of these methods of building are successful - and yes - it takes time to build a good business. Thank you for sharing your hard earned "secrets" with those of us enjoying the benefits of network marketing and home based businesses!"

B.J. Stromme
District Manager II, Jafra Cosmetics

Your Best Year In Network Marketing

How To Achieve The Financial Success You Deserve

Mark Yarnell

Your Best Year In Network Marketing: How To Achieve The Financial Success You Deserve

Copyright 2002 Mark Yarnell

FIRST EDITION
ISBN: 1-879706-94-6

Paper Chase Press books may be purchased for educational purposes, business or sales promotional use. For information, please write: Special Markets Dept., Paper Chase Press, 5721 Magazine Street, Suite 152, New Orleans LA, 70115, or call: 800/460-8604.

Cover Design: Winky Wheeler, Portland, OR

"Every formula for success shinks in significance in the presence of one simple yet profound notion: Leaders demonstrate what is possible."
Mark Yarnell

For Valerie, of course.

ACKNOWLEDGMENTS

I'd like to personally thank everyone who has
contributed immeasurably to my 51 years of life.

Thanks... You know who you are.
Especially I'd like to thank Christine Perkio
for countless hours of editing and typing,
and Amy Yarnell, my daughter and
greatest worldly contribution.

Contents

Contents

Preface

LIFE IS GREAT. I'VE JUST FINISHED MY THREE BEST YEARS in the last thirty. I have great friends, a wonderful family, plenty of money, and a new business venture. But there's one little piece of unfinished business I must tend to. I can't lean on past success or outdated books. Now that three of my other books are obsolete (excluding, of course, *Self-Wealth*), I decided to undertake this definitive new work you are about to read. *Your First Year in Network Marketing* continues to sell at a record pace, but I'm spending too much time retracting concepts that were valid several years ago yet make no sense today. Some authors in network marketing who are only motivated by money, are content to promote outdated materials. But I am not such a writer. For one thing, I'm not doing it for the money. I have plenty. I've written this book because I want the truth to be known about the current state of affairs in the networking industry.

It only makes sense to upgrade and change old concepts which can and do slow down serious network marketing professionals. Some methods that worked back in the early '90s are now stumbling blocks for those who want to thrive in this industry. I get calls from people every week who wonder why something they have read in *Your First Year In Network Marketing* doesn't work. I explain to them that many of the concepts are no longer valid and most question why I would not write a new book outlining the most effective approach to success in this field. Well, here it is. I've had a blast writing it.

My last books were survival manuals. Unfortunately, the ideas have taken very few people beyond survival to dramatic wealth. Countless networkers have told me that they enjoyed the books, but not one networker has thanked me for helping him/her become a millionaire. That's about to change.

In this new book, I'm getting down to business. My main objective is to replace obsolete concepts from my previous books and provide a forthright approach to help serious networkers learn how to create substantial wealth. I want you to experience your best year in network marketing-not merely survive your first. If your goal is to earn a million dollars a year or more, and to enhance your life and the lives of others, this is the book for you. If you want to read cute stories about the humorous failures that tend to occur in a new networker's life, by all means, read my previous books. But please don't call me and complain about obsolete concepts if you insist only on reading the stuff I wrote in the last century.

Yarnell, You're Crazy!

A couple of my friends have told me that I'm an idiot to update my concepts in a new book. One close acquaintance recently said, "Yarnell, you're crazy! You're making a killing off your last book. If it ain't broke, don't fix it!" The problem is that many of the ideas in the last book are broke. For example, in-home presentations are history. Small meetings are a dinosaur approach to building a business. Rejection is an inevitable fact of life, but everyone already knows that without reading the many pages I commit to the subject in the previous book. The old ads I taught are now ineffective. Some of the people I interviewed while researching my last book have failed or quit. Internet recruiting is now being attempted by many networkers and should be addressed.

In this new book, you'll learn from some of the genuine legends in our industry. Most have been with one company for a decade or more and they understand what you need to know to make the big dollars. I've included their stories and guidance to inform you and not merely to entertain. This book truly is a roadmap to long-term wealth and not just a survival manual for new distributors. I had other things to do besides write another book, but at least from now on I don't have to listen to people complain about obsolete concepts from the past. You might say that my motives were selfish given the amount of time I've spent admitting that other books and articles are outdated. However, it was so time- consuming answering calls from failing distributors that it became necessary to sit down and invest a few months in an updated book about professional network marketing. I suppose I'll have to do it again in five or six years, but for now, this is current. Don't bug me until we're closer to 2008.

This book is succinct. It wasn't written for your leisure reading enjoyment. I want you earning at least $100,000 a month so I don't have to take your phone call in six months and listen to why they just repossessed your car. The last time I wrote a book it was because the publisher offered me a big pile of money before I ever wrote one page. This time I've written a book that no one had to pay me to write. This time I offer you a labor of love based on hard hitting facts designed to help you rise to income levels you never even dreamed possible. These concepts will work-if you do.

The good news is, if you follow these concepts faithfully for the next couple of years, you won't have to waste your money on "how to" books ever again. You'll have succeeded.

If you're ready to stop thinking about growing rich and start doing it, this book is your ticket. Your first day in professional networking begins when you start reading chapter one. The number of years you may have been in the business is inconsequential. Today you begin anew. Each chapter is another step in your march toward dramatic wealth. Forget what you've been taught. When you succeed, it won't be because you've duplicated me. You will succeed because you've learned how to exploit your own inherent potential and capabilities.

Do not skip one chapter and do not proceed to the next chapter until you've applied the one you've just read. Don't attempt a short cut. If you find yourself mentally arguing with me or tempted to skip a step just consider this: I've earned over 15 million dollars in one company and you haven't. Your way hasn't worked or you'd be sitting on the beach reading *Islands* magazine rather than this book.

Why Many People Fail

The reason most people fail is that they would rather win than be right. I spent years with a person like that. This isn't some battle in which you get to argue with my ideas. You're in one of the most promising fields in free enterprise and you aren't getting any younger. Your family probably doesn't have a fraction of what they deserve and it's not because you're stupid. In fact, it may be because you're too smart for your own good. Just this once, please LISTEN and then TAKE ACTION!

Don't worry, once you're earning over a million dollars a year, you'll get all the credit. No one even has to know that you've read this book or followed my system. You get to be the hero, but first you have to earn it by having the courage to stuff your ego long enough to pay attention to something you didn't create. The hardest thing I ever did was shut up long enough to listen to someone who knew more than I did. But I did. Now it's your turn. Once you've read the introduction, turn to Chapter One and begin.

This Book Will Stir Controversy

This book will be somewhat controversial because I'm going to tell the truth about the way some people operate in the network marketing industry. It's about time. I'm also going to teach distributors in older companies how to become wealthy by reinventing them like several Shaklee folks are doing. Some companies will resent these facts because they wish to remain in comfort zones where they can keep regulators at arms-length by discouraging their distributors from drawing attention to themselves. Distributors are independent entrepreneurs who need to be reinventing themselves every few years in order to avoid stagnation. It's up to those of us in the field, and not up to corporate leaders.

This book is dedicated to those individuals who are courageous enough to take control of their own destinies and either build a dynasty in their current company or seek out a new one which will allow them to do so. Nothing is sadder than those poor souls who willingly become trapped in capital preservation in an unlimited field like MLM because corporate leaders impose rules designed to keep distributors "in place."

One of the greatest causes of failure in professional networking results from company owners who are content with a few million dollars in annual profits. Corporate owners launch companies with the original intention of mass-distributing products, and spend the next thirty years imposing rules and regulations that tie their distributors' hands. A good example of this is that MLM companies with good products and compensation plans don't have to force their distributors to sign non-compete contracts in order to keep them involved.

Networkers often lose their enthusiasm and spend their careers trying to protect a few thousand dollars a month when they could be earning millions. Or they quit and join money games that fold in six months. You'll learn another option in this book.

I've made things simple in this book because you need to be recruiting and selling products rather than reading. Each chapter ends with an assignment or summary to complete before moving on to the next chapter. So follow the directions.

Introduction

EVERY GREAT NETWORKER WAS A LOUSY NETWORKER FIRST. Yet those of us who manage to hang in there long enough and work hard enough to earn huge incomes are frequently granted rock star status. Some people want to have their pictures taken with us at public appearances while others actually hang back from the crowd as if they were unworthy to approach us. Some leaders contribute to their own mythical status by showing off their money with all the toys they own. They purchase late model sports cars, huge homes and boats and strut around at conventions like dictators of third world nations. I did. I hate to admit it, but I did just that.

While it seems natural to display our wealth in a world in which money is given so much emphasis, it's important for MLM leaders to present both sides of the MLM story. We all made mistakes that can and should be avoided by others who aspire to our levels of success. This became clearer to me as I traveled around delivering keynote speeches at company conventions in the late 1990's. Those who are proud to have survived their first year but still wonder when they'll have their best year, generally approach me. Many readers survive their first year battles only to wonder when they can actually pay their bills and earn a respectable income in network marketing.

One Year Experience Multiplied

Unfortunately it's possible to have one year of experience five times, instead of five years of growth and progress unless you continue to grow and learn. I want this year to be your best year. It's not particularly easy, once a man or woman has had considerable success, to go back to the early days and recount embarrassing failures. The tendency is to point to those things which resulted in success. Unfortunately, when legends refuse to disclose their failures, others are doomed to repeat them.

My best year in network marketing was not the year that I made the most money. Financial prosperity is just part of the equation. My best year occurred when I calmed down long enough to experience genuine serenity and balance. My best year resulted from a mindset, not a Mercedes. Indeed it could have occurred half a decade sooner with a little strategic planning and wisdom. Wisdom I now present in this book.

Clara McDermott, in my opinion the all time greatest MLM matriarch, gave me very sound advice my first year when she insisted that I not spend a fortune on an extravagant lifestyle until I'd been successful for at least two years. Of course I paid absolutely no attention to her. My mentor, Richard Kall, told me to invest my money wisely. I didn't. Several outstanding leaders advised me not to travel around the country conducting meetings. So I did. One year, as an incentive to my downline, I had a recruiting contest in which the winner received a new Lexus. Everyone in my upline told me I was a fool to do so. They were right.

My friends and family said I was too obsessed; that I was working entirely too many hours a week and that I would eventually burn out. I did. When I finally reached a point of absolute exhaustion, instead of creating balance in my life, I quit for an entire year against the protests of those who were more experienced and my organization began to deteriorate from the top down just like they had warned me it would.

Imagine waking up at age 40 with an airplane, three mansions, a wardrobe of designer clothes, a summer chalet in Switzerland, more money than you can possibly spend, a pile of books, tapes and major magazine articles to your credit and every award available in the entire MLM industry, only to discover that your life is empty. I had literally become so busy making a living that I'd forgotten to make a life. It took a decade of painful self-reflection and dramatic change to alter my course. But at age 51, I finally understand the importance of balance, serenity and prosperity. That is not to say that I've somehow "arrived" or that there won't be additional challenges in the future. But my best year in network marketing could have been my third or fourth instead of my tenth. It is that possibility which I hope to help you realize through this book.

Your Best Year In Network Marketing

Yes, your best year in network marketing will occur when you're finally out of debt and earning enough to make ends meet comfortably. It will be a year in which you are able to strike a balance between diligent effort and time freedom. Your best year will be when you feel serene and confident, successful and fulfilled. The pressure will be off not because you're earning more than you can spend, but because you realize that no matter what happens you can always recover. Your best year in network marketing could come in the first or third year but it will be punctuated by contentment and you will spend considerable time with those whom you most love. You will perhaps donate some time and or money to a worthy cause and you'll stop reading menus from right to left.

Your best year in network marketing will be the end of erroneous prioritizing, self-destructive habits and hollow relationships. You'll slow down long enough to figure out what's really meaningful and what isn't and you'll begin to revisit the dreams and aspirations of your youth. You'll begin to write or paint, you'll climb into an airplane for your first flight instruction, or go back to college to enjoy a few of those courses you've always wanted to take.

Perhaps more important than anything else, your best year in network marketing will occur when countless people in your organization recognize that you're one of them — filled with the same hopes and dreams, fears and foibles. When the world knows you're approachable in spite of your success and accessible in spite of your prestige — that's when your life will begin to make sense. One of the shortest distances in life is from our head to our heart and it's a trip we should all make daily.

MLM: The Great Equalizer

Network marketing is the great equalizer in free enterprise because
removes the numerous prejudices that block many from rising to their
fullest potential in traditional business. Lack of education, sexuality, colo
age, creed, appearance and other impediments to social and financia
mobility have no power in network marketing. We all begin at the top c
our own companies and succeed by elevating others. Unlike most zer
sum games, everyone wins in our industry. But the real adult report card i
fulfillment, not cash, and fulfillment is a by-product of "other-directed
activities, a sense of balance, and self-respect.

Of course, I'm proceeding here from the assumption that you have a
IQ of over 100 and you have already recognized that some people ar
clueless. One of the things you will learn your very first week i
professional networking is that not all of the squirrels are in the trees
However, we'll assume that you are reasonably intelligent. Therefore, I'r
not going to waste a bunch of valuable time attempting to verify the fac
that network marketing, (or MLM, as most people hate to call it), is
legitimate business. If your next-door neighbor and business associates ar
still using the old pyramid argument from the 60s and 70s-move or
Anyone with half a brain recognizes the stupidity of working for a salary c
hourly wage when they can multiply their efforts through ten thousan
others.

It used to be easy for any pseudo-author to write a best-selling book b
devoting 250 pages to an in-depth analysis of why network marketing is
real business. Our entire industry was once screaming for credibilit
There are dozens of those books out there and if they seem similar it'
because many were ghost written by the same guy. That's another story.

The reason those books are irrelevant now is that MLM has been
credible profession for two decades. Those who refuse to accept that fac
are hopelessly stuck in the 70s. Those who keep trying to recruit nev
distributors by arguing that MLM isn't a pyramid are years behind th
curve. Any sixth grader now has at least one classmate whose MLM
parents' lifestyles allow both to attend all PTA meetings and school events
Chances are that most children with two medical doctor parents hav
grown up in a neighborhood where the only home bigger than their

belongs to a person who's been in MLM for 10 years. I still get the prospecting question: "Is this MLM?" Back in the 80s, I responded with a well-calculated speech about passive residual income and an answer designed to defend our industry. Today I answer, "Of course it's MLM! You don't think you could earn this kind of money as a surgeon do you?"

Are You Among The Clueless?

The only people who don't understand the power of professional network marketing are hopelessly incompetent. Some are patently incapable of succeeding in our business if they don't even understand the potential of our industry in the first place. They are what I lovingly call "clueless." Of course not all of those who reject your recruiting ovations are clueless. A few are simply dedicated and truly enjoy their chosen profession. Many are scared because there's no exit strategy. Anyone can be laid off or downsized in spite of their MBA or years of loyalty to one corporation. Even doctors can defend their mediocre incomes by blaming it all on HMOs. But once a person learns how to pick a legitimate networking company that's marketing an effective product she's not going to be able to point the finger at anyone else but herself if she doesn't have an AMEX platinum in short order.

Of course that's not to say that people don't fail regularly in our industry. But usually they pick a company selling something they don't really believe in-like rat poison or snot guards. Then they put two thousand dollars into some unbalanced binary created by someone who's done seven years on a Ricco Racketeering charge. I have no sympathy for people selling products that they can't discuss in church or those who sign up in deals that they know are more of a gamble than NASDAQ. If a thousand people join a stupid deal, it's still a stupid deal.

Some Assumptions Before We Get Started

Apart from normal intelligence, I'm also proceeding from the assumption that you are interested in building prosperity with purpose. I assume you got into professional networking because you found a patented product or service that changes people's lives and you know the backgrounds of the company leaders. I'm assuming that you understand the comp plan and that your company will allow you to become wealthy without jumping through a bunch of hoops so long as you build an organization that does legitimate volume, even if you only sponsor one winner.

I'm making the assumption that you've joined a company that's somewhat mature but doesn't yet have a million distributors, in 30 countries. I'm also assuming that your company has the capital and ability to expand into numerous foreign markets in order to profit from our global economy. I trust that you already understand that you cannot peel two potatoes at the same time, nor can you achieve dramatic wealth by doing two or three MLM deals simultaneously. In 15 years, throughout hundreds of interviews, I've never met one legend who made big money by working more than one program at the same time. Those folks who think they can minimize their risk by joining four companies would be much better off jumping barefoot into a box of light bulbs. Or, even better, they could go to Vegas and feed four slot machines at the same time.

The reason that I'm proceeding from those basic assumptions is so that I can spend my time writing about things of substance. If you don't even know how to evaluate a well-capitalized ground floor opportunity, honest comp plan, legitimate product or ethical management team, this book will probably not help you. Or worse, if you understand those things yet persist in leading decent people into money games, this information won't work for you in the long term.

This book is intended to help serious network marketing professionals prepare for their best year in this business. These professionals are prepared to learn from those who have succeeded and then do what it takes to earn incredible incomes-perhaps exceeding a million dollars a year. I've never met any person who retired from a J.O.B. or respected profession with a pension of a million dollars a year. It's one thing to scrape, save and sacrifice so that after 40 or 50 years you can have assets like *The Millionaire Next Door*. But what our industry offers is an opportunity to work 10% or 20% as long and then have a cash flow of a million dollars each year for life.

The reason that this book is for the serious networker is that flakes never make it to the top. They jump from deal to deal until everyone knows their game or they are so exhausted they've got to resort to dot com I.P.O.s, or Las Vegas. Of course if you are a flake you might want to admit it promptly, make amends to everyone you've hurt, turn your life over to a Higher Networker, and begin attending F.A. meetings. There is hope.

The Aspiring Networker

I've also written this book for future network marketing professionals who care about a straightforward, honest, and legitimate business system. It's time to teach people how to do it right. I've got a list of character defects as long as your arm, but one of them isn't greed-motivated deception. I don't want scumbags to be able to use this book in order to build lousy companies at the expense of innocent victims. No one in any Internet gifting game or binary pyramid scam will be sending this book to friends for Christmas. In fact, when was the last time an author admitted that his former books were obsolete even though they were selling hundreds of thousands of copies at that very time? My other three books are obsolete. There, I did it.

Sometimes I wish books were like cars. If I could recall all of mine, I would. Unfortunately, an ex-publisher and an ex-wife don't always see it my way. That's why they are ex's. When big bucks are at stake, few people are willing to take the road less traveled. But, that's another story too, and one I refuse to tell because the best revenge is a life well lived.

I've enjoyed writing this book because it's the truth and it's current. Now that it's available I am not assuming responsibility for past concepts which are, today, woefully inadequate.

So, let's get down to business. Forget about everything you've heard and move to Chapter One. If you know you're involved in a money game, first get out there and pick a company and product about which you are both proud and passionate and then come back to this book. It doesn't do any good to attempt to build something in some silly market that probably won't be around in another year.

I've met dozens of decent people who have blown their credibility by jumping into five deals in a row for greed-motivated reasons.

Make a five-year commitment before reading Chapter One and never look at another company no matter how slick some recruiter sounds. This entire book will provide you with serious principles you need to earn millions. But they will do you no good if you pick a screwball company. There is nothing unique about me-too product companies that promote front-end loading with huge sign-up packages. Some people pretend that they are in a "real deal," but most of us know intuitively if we are joining a scam. Don't do that no matter how tempted if you want this book to work for you. Even if your company has been around for over a decade, we'll explore a simple and innovative system for building a new network of enthusiastic recruits.

So let's go. Today you can begin your best year in network marketing. And the good news is, it's not just a way to make a living. It's the best way to make a life.

CHAPTER ONE

Goals Worth Pursuing

"Most of us stop short of our potential, once our primary needs have been met."

I USED TO WONDER IF FINANCIALLY SUCCESSFUL PEOPLE had anything in common – apart from being successful, of course. Doctors, lawyers, best-selling authors, professional athletes, actors, affluent business people – what do they have in common? I discovered, as I began interviewing them for various books and articles, that they generally have two things in common. First, they are very focused goal setters. And second, they give their money away to good causes – causes for the benefit of others with far less.

Of course the media ignores most of their giving because "good news is no news." The media is more interested in creating hype over Donald Trump's latest sexual liaisons than the millions he has donated to the Boy Scouts. Bill Gates is more noted for his monopoly fight with the government than for the billions he has donated to education and African AIDS projects. Oprah Winfrey gets more press when she's being sued by the beef ranchers than for programs she supports to aid single women and their children. It seems that unless a notable person like a Mother Theresa or an Albert Schweitzer is willing to move to impoverished countries and spend their last two decades in service, we seldom hear about their meaningful goals.

A Goal Bigger Than Yourself

I also discovered that along with goal setting, most financially successful people share another thing in common: they set goals bigger than themselves. They aren't motivated by goals that are strictly money oriented. Admittedly, it is entertaining to learn of how "such and so" was able to overcome incredible odds, and end up becoming enormously rich. This is part of our culture; it's called The American Dream. And there is nothing wrong with that.

But the goals these highly successful people set for themselves usually involve meaningful endeavors that are not related to making money. Some of these people are interested in education, while others are passionate about the homeless problem or preserving our environment. The fact is, I learned that life for most highly successful people is more about the legacy they leave than the car they drive (although most of them drive nice cars anyway). My impression is that most of these people were only able to truly enjoy success once they directed their energies towards altruistic objectives. Because, in our heart of hearts, beyond our personal needs, most of us find life much more gratifying when we help others. To be sure, we all like nice things, but most of us realize that meaning comes more from unselfishly assisting others than from giving ourselves nicer cars and bigger homes.

Donald Black is a relationship expert I know who often challenges his audiences at lectures by asking them this question: "How would you feel if tomorrow morning you woke up and learned that you had just won the $250 million lottery, but you were the only person left on earth?" Obviously his point is the need for emphasis on our relationships and on sharing what we have with others rather than living for material things only. Of course, there are some people who are strictly greed-motivated, but social psychologists have discovered that even selfish people often have goals that benefit others. In other words, they have *meaningful goals*.

"Meaningful goals are more meaningful than goals."

Other-Directed Goals

I call meaningful goals, *other*-directed goals. I've been a goal setter since my mother introduced me to Napoleon Hill's work thirty-five years ago. As I consider my former successes, I attribute many of them to goal setting. My bestsellers, the Lotus Esprit, the home in Switzerland, the airplane, the boat: they were all goals and achieving them was gratifying. But the real secret is this: when I had "just" those goals, I never succeeded in achieving any of them. I wanted all those things, but they eluded me until I created two meaningful goals that involved the lives of others. That's when I learned three important facts that have been verified countless times.

First, big homes and fancy cars don't bring a fraction of the fulfillment that unselfish sharing brings. Second, it's much easier to give away money than manage it. Third, those who can't really conceptualize big enough goals to stretch themselves will never have big money except by some fluke or chance (which almost never happens). Let's look at those facts in reverse.

How My Goals Grew

I grew up in Missouri farmland where I thought riches were a bicycle and two clothespins that held playing cards to the spokes so that my bike sounded like a motorcycle (at least in my mind). When bleeding madras shirts were "in," Mom made me one, but the sleeves were too short, so I added to my concept of riches a store-bought madras shirt that had sufficiently long sleeves.

Of course, in my twenties, the goals became greater, but the thought of earning $100,000 or more per month never entered my head. Therein lies the first problem. Most of us can never profit from the unlimited income potential of networking because our primary needs are met by an income of substantially less than a million dollars a year. Personal goals involving material wealth are seldom very large.

Why I've Made More Money Than Most

One of the most frequent questions I encountered at lectures was why so few people in my former organization earned as much as I did. Was it because I was better skilled or was it because my business building system cannot be duplicated? It was neither. The reason was that, shortly before I became involved in network marketing, I created, for the first time in my life, a meaningful goal bigger than myself. My associates couldn't imagine such huge goals.

I met a guy in Austin who had figured out a way to help poor people and prisoners escape alcoholism and drug addiction. That excited me. Addiction had become such a big business that only those with a good health plan or $25,000 were admitted into treatment. Yet a huge percentage of homeless people and felons are addicts and have no place to turn. Without the goal to fund that project, I could have quite easily stopped working when my income was $6,000 a month. Instead, I kept building until I was earning enough money to do some good. The first logical reason for creating a meaningful goal far beyond our own personal needs is that most of us will stop short of our potential once our primary needs have been met.

The second reason will probably seem goofy but it's accurate. Managing $30,000 or more a month is impossible unless you are a trained money manager. The reason so many people stop short of the big income in MLM is that they figure out quite rapidly that managing it is a nightmare. Big money attracts every con artist and carnival barker in America. Nine out of ten big investment deals turn out to be scams. You soon learn that when you've got money, real estate is always in a "seller's market" when you buy, and a "buyer's market" when you sell. Most upstarts and IPOs go under for inexplicable and unlucky reasons-especially the "sure deals." Investment brokers have an uncanny way of investing your capital in deals that could have "never failed" but did. In fact, if you're like me, you may even wind up tucking your money safely away in one hundred year old savings and loans that just happen to go under a month later.

The Folly of Wall Street

If you think Vegas is a gamble, wait until you spend a few months on Wall Street. Of course, brokers will tell you that your money is safe in America's grand old stock market, but let's use a little common sense. If stockbrokers are paid to make trades whether you lose money or make a profit and billionaire investment experts can win whether the market goes up or down...well, shucks folks. Do you maybe suppose that novice investors like you and me might have an unfair disadvantage in the Wall Street game?

Here's my point. Once your check gets to a certain amount, every idiot and crook in your immediate environment has a new idea. And as Peter Frampton remarked recently after being unable to account for the whereabouts of seventy-four million dollars he had earned through the sales of his albums, "I'm not rich, but all my managers are!" I don't care what anyone tells you, it's easier to give your money away than it is to try to save it.

To be safe, you'll want to tuck away a few hundred thousand in several banks, but if you're smart you'll figure out a meaningful goal and give away most of your money. For God's sake, don't get sucked into the tax savings scams. Pay your taxes and pay them on time. People who screw the IRS go to jail. Get it?

Emptiness In Materialism

Finally, material possessions do not bring joy or fulfillment. Most people who have never experienced the problems of a gilded cage argue about that point. People tell me; "Gee, Yarnell, I'd like to experience that problem just once." That's because they haven't.

In the final analysis, you will ultimately be just about as happy as you make up your mind to be, at whatever your income level. It will have absolutely nothing to do with money or things. If your marriage stinks, a new boat or car won't change the smell. If you're drinking too much and you move to a bigger home, you'll simply have more rooms in which to be drunk. If your dad hates you and you give him a trip to Bermuda, he'll hate you from the island. If you aren't spending quality time with your children and you give them new sports cars, you'll never spend any time with them.

Nothing brings more real fulfillment than creating and achieving meaningful goals designed to unselfishly help those who can't help themselves or those who truly need the help. The recognition, even if it is anonymous, is beyond your wildest dreams.

"The fact is, if you can't figure out some specific motives for earning a million dollars or more a year...you never will."

Define Specific Meaningful Goals

So the purpose of this first chapter is to give you the master secret of the rich and famous: goals. And preferably help you set specific, meaningful goals. Sit down right now and create several *meaningful* goals. Write them out to look at, even if they seem a little far-fetched right now.

The fact is, if you can't figure out some specific motives for earning a million dollars or more a year...you never will. You simply won't summon the drive and the passion to fulfill the goal. Nearly everyone has some passion, some pet interest that can be of benefit to others. Look around our world and pick something about which you can become passionate. Initially you may want to just determine a dollar amount to stick in a special account for the specific purpose of eventually helping others. But don't wait long to identify specific goals.

While it's virtually impossible to invest $30,000 a month intelligently, it's easy to give away that much anonymously. The more personally passionate you are, the better the goals will be. Trust me. DO NOT move on to Chapter Two until you've spent some quality time in this meaningful goal exercise.

If you ignore this first step, the other concepts you're about to learn will be moot. It simply makes no sense to attempt to earn more money than you need, more money than you can manage, and more money than will make you happy. That's precisely why very few people ever make the huge incomes in our industry.

True Path To Riches

Unless you are pathologically greedy, or just lucky, you must have meaningful goals or you will never earn more than a few thousand a month regardless of how great your company or product may be. And even if you do, you'll eventually wind up depressed, disillusioned and miserable when it becomes obvious that material wealth is all just a grand illusion.

If you think that a "goal bigger than yourself" is merely the ramblings of a deluded former minister, think again. I've rubbed shoulders with rich and famous people from many different countries and backgrounds and the one thing I found they all had in common was a goal bigger than themselves. Ted Turner inherited his dad's billboard company that automatically made him a millionaire. But that was not enough. Ted wanted to develop a global TV news system for the world, particularly for nations who could not get the news at all. And he wanted to use his money to improve the environment-he personally pledged to give $100 million dollars a year to the United Nations for the next ten years just for that purpose. As a multi-billionaire, of course, Ted can contribute any way he wants.

Bill Gates had it in his heart to improve the educational system. He's the richest man in the world and is doing what he can. George Soros was the man who made a billion dollars over night, literally, in the world stock trade – so he could help the former Eastern Block of countries develop businesses. His personal financial contribution and management has literally changed the lives of tens of thousands of people across Europe. Wendy's Hamburgers founder, Dave Thomas was an orphan who wanted to find a way to help orphans – he's a multi-millionaire and helps orphans. And the list goes on and on.

You must begin your best year in network marketing by deciding to give more than you could ever need to spend on yourself or you'll never get what you're worth. Remember: meaningful goals are more meaningful than just money-oriented goals. To make truly big money, a million or more a year, you need the necessary passion, drive and reason to make that type of money. That is the foundation upon which you are about to build a future beyond your greatest expectations. Ignore the foundation and you'll only fall short.

SUMMARY

Many people come to network marketing thinking that this is a path to quick and easy riches. The fact is, that is far from the truth. Network marketing, like any other business, requires a great deal of commitment and effort. But before you get started, it is important to define your goals.

- To truly earn big money, you must define goals worth pursuing, or what I call meaningful goals.

- Extraordinarily successful people have one significant thing in common – they achieve financial goals which enable them to achieve the goals they truly value, which is to help others. They pursue such causes as helping the poor, investing in AIDS research, creating a better educational system, improving the environment, and so on.

- I have introduced you to the idea that material wealth can never truly satisfy in the way that giving of yourself to others can.

- Most of us will stop short of our potential, once our primary needs have been met. If you want to really do something meaningful, you need to look beyond your immediate material needs.

- Those who cannot conceptualize having big money – in excess of a one million dollars a year – probably will never earn that much money. True, there are exceptions to this, but those are only a few.

CHAPTER TWO

Innovation Vs. Duplication

"Great leaders always innovate, they don't duplicate."

I'LL NEVER FORGET HOW SHOCKED I WAS when one of my best leaders decided to leave our company and start his own venture. It wasn't his decision to sell his downline that disturbed me. Lives change and people move on. It was the statements he made about me while attempting to recruit distributors into his new deal. He said that essentially he was the main reason I had succeeded and that seventy percent of my entire downline was under him. The reason it bothered me was that he was right. Not only was he correct about that, but he also went further to suggest that he had never even duplicated my system. He claimed he had done it all his way. Again, it disturbed me because he was absolutely right.

"The closer I examined my organization, the more I noticed that every real leader had his or her own system."

Of course he never disclosed the fact that one couple on his front line accounted for over 70 percent of his volume and that this couple had never duplicated anything either he or I taught them. No one in that entire leg of my downline had more than one really strong downline organization. That's the way MLM works. In fact, that's ironically the biggest complaint about binary compensation plans. All you need in a binary is two front line people, but the trick in some companies is to have them both balanced and successful. I hear people in binaries complaining that most of their volume is coming from one "runaway" leg. Most people can't even build two strong legs, a fact which occurred years ago to analytical corporate types who then setup money games that looked simple because they required only two legs. More on that later, now back to my story.

What disturbed me most, the closer I examined my organization, was that every real leader had his or her own system. In fact, so did I. Against the protests of my best upline leaders, I began running ads in the sales section of my local newspaper. It was those ads that pulled the most distributors. The only structure I followed was really not a system at all. Richard Kall said, "get twenty customers before you start recruiting." I did. Then he said, "go wide fast. If you don't recruit one new front line each day you're failing!" So I made it a point to get one distributor each day, whatever it took. And finally he taught me that; "the life blood of your organization is the new blood." Consequently, I spent my time looking for new distributors rather than attempting to manage or motivate those who had already signed up.

Those were the principles Richard taught me and I'll always consider him a genius. The systems to implement them, I invented. And not only did I invent my own recruiting strategies, but so did my best downline leaders in spite of my "duplication" battle cry.

Two Truths of MLM

There are two fundamental truths in MLM, which most legends are willing to admit privately but bristle about in public. First, nobody is really a legendary dynamo singularly responsible for building a huge group. It's a team effort and those of us who work really hard will eventually blunder into one or two other people who work really hard and so on. Second, nobody ever really duplicates anybody else. Each of us brings our own unique personality, competence, ethics and work habits to the table. A great leader will provide certain objectives like two retail customers a month and one new distributor a day to new recruits, and help those new distributors develop a set of strategies that best fits their personal abilities.

My best year in network marketing began with the realization that I need never again be angry with other leaders in my organization for refusing to duplicate my system. For years there were undercurrents of anger, back-biting and frustration in my organization. And I'm sorry to say that much of it began at the very top. That's right, I was the culprit. After all, I had built a dynasty so how dare anyone challenge my authority. I entered into childish gossip with people who called me to tattle on their uplines for not duplicating my system. Some of my more daring leaders actually had the audacity to create their own audio tapes instead of using mine. And horror of horrors, some of their sales aids were better than mine. My whole life was about putting out brushfires and arguing with entrepreneurs who dared to ignore the almighty Yarnell system.

General Manager of the Universe

Everything in life became much more enjoyable for me the year that I decided to resign as general manager of the universe. It all happened in the most unlikely manner. It was 1992 and I had just accepted an opportunity as a regular contributing editor for *Success* magazine. My objective was to interview various legends and write articles about how they had built huge organizations. I had received the unprecedented invitation to sit in on an advanced training session of one of our industry's top distributors in America's undisputed king of MLM companies. It was unprecedented for me to be there because not even leaders from other organizations within that same company were granted admission. I was an outsider.

When I got to the door of the huge banquet hall, I went through a security clearance worthy of a participant in a U.S. Presidential Pentagon meeting. Men with walkie-talkies communicated my name back and forth until a backstage security leader received permission from The Legend himself to admit me. I entered a banquet hall with some 5,000 cheering participants and was escorted to VIP seating near the front. Thirty minutes later than the planned start time, the lights dimmed and an overweight, fifty-ish guy ran on the stage to applause so thunderous I feared a possible building collapse. I actually found myself getting sucked into the mass hysteria, clapping as if I were at an "Elvis Returns" concert.

For the next several hours, I watched intently, and even took notes, as The Legend railed about the moral decay in America. From Madonna to Michael Jackson, the speaker attacked numerous celebrities and what he viewed as their blatant efforts to bring America to its moral knees. After criticizing artists, he spent a couple of hours attacking left-wing politicians, and about an hour in what could only be considered a Christian altar call.

The final hour was supposed to be an actual demonstration of how to conduct an in-home presentation. He selected two eager kids to come up on stage and play the roles of a young married couple. For some curious reason, he picked two young men and asked one to portray a woman. After their giddiness subsided, obviously the result of being so close to the great man, they began to answer each of his questions as if they were scripted. No objections. Just two supposedly "critical thinking" young people who salivated at the prospect of joining the company. The mock presentation lasted an hour and a half during which time The Legend did little more than crack impromptu witticisms, (none of which were remotely funny), to the squeals and laughter of a Stepford audience.

When the advanced training was over, I had absolutely nothing of substance to report in my *Success* magazine article. However, I was whisked away in a caravan of limos to the airport and told that I would perhaps have five precious minutes alone with The Legend before his flight left Dallas.

"None of the leaders had ever duplicated anything they had learned from their legendary upline."

Our meeting never transpired. Such a huge crowd had assembled at the departure gate that no one except his top leaders could get within ten feet of him. As we waved goodbye and his plane pushed back from the terminal I walked passed a bar in which I noticed three or four of his inner circle who had assembled furtively in a back corner over beer and Bloody Marys. After explaining to them who I was and that I was there to write an article for *Success* magazine about their organization, they invited me to join them. For the next couple of hours, as the alcohol lowered their walls of resistance, I learned the truth about their company's remarkable success.

According to them, the advanced training session I had just attended was called "Upline Edification." It had absolutely nothing to do with duplication or education. None of the leaders had ever duplicated anything they had learned from their legendary upline, nor did any of them have the slightest idea how the people in their upline had actually succeeded. They pointed out that once a person has risen to that guy's level, he has earned the right to be exalted. He is also allowed to create his own audio tapes at a base cost of twenty-five cents a tape and sell them to his own downline for five dollars each. No one at that table could offer me an insight into any system, which had resulted in such a huge downline beyond the fact that their leader had been in the business for twenty-six years and had recruited several hundred frontline distributors. Each of them did, however, offer me their own system for success, none of which even remotely resembled the others. The key, they said, was hard work, loyalty, meeting attendance, tape club membership and upline adulation as a morale booster.

In the end I was spared the embarrassment of writing a shallow article when The Legend refused to approve the photograph

Success had selected of him. At the time, *Success* magazine had an editorial policy that layout people were allowed to select their own spontaneous portraits of their subjects. The Legend insisted that he would provide his own portrait (no doubt a leaner, younger version of himself). The editors declined and the article was never published.

Now, I don't believe for one minute that we ever elevate ourselves by denigrating others. My purpose in sharing that illustration is merely to make the point that duplication played no role in the growth of one of our industry's premiere organizations. And far be it from me to suggest that a person who has dedicated twenty-six years of his life to one downline in one company is not worthy of some recognition. He probably deserves a gold metal, or a plaque or something, for loyalty and perseverance.

De-emphasize Duplication

What I am saying is: let's face facts and stop giving legitimacy to the absurd concept of duplication. It's entrepreneurial innovation, not organizational duplication that works.

My best year in network marketing began with the decision to respect other entrepreneurial leaders in my organization for their own unique and innovative talents.   The year that I began to acknowledge and applaud each leader's creative system instead of demanding that they follow mine, my income doubled. I would no longer interfere and try to force people to adopt my techniques. Once I left people to do their own techniques, they did just fine. The fact is, some people operate at different level than others. You have super performers, you have slower performers, and you have every variation in between. It's just human nature.

When my company opened in Europe I went to London to recruit new distributors. Most of the "big guns" went to Germany, but I didn't want to deal with the language barrier so I chose England as my next stop.   In England, I met an impoverished couple who couldn't afford their own car. Together we figured out a recruiting strategy that highlighted their talents and they went to work. Within six months they had risen to the highest level in our company, setting a record for all of Europe which still hasn't been surpassed. Their system was not one I would have ever been able to duplicate, but it worked for them.

Big Al Decries Duplication

To give credit where credit is due, Tom Schrieder tried to teach me the folly of duplication years before I finally figured it out. Known as Big Al to most of the industry, Tom is one of the funniest most self-deprecating leaders I've ever met. He's truly a legend and those who haven't heard his tapes or read his materials should do so. His object lesson in the folly of duplication occurred at an Upline Masters Seminar during a panel question and answer session in which we both participated back in 1990. Richard Brooke, President of Oxyfresh, and Sandy Ellsburg, industry consultant, were the other two panelists and it was our job to field and answer questions from the audience.

A question about duplication arose and I began to wax eloquently on the subject. When I had finished a brilliant oration, the same subject was put to Big Al. He said, "duplication is not quite as important as Yarnell and others believe, in my opinion. Let's say that you're at the doctor's office for a physical exam and upon leaving you accidentally back your car into a new Mercedes. The irate driver climbs out and as you're exchanging insurance verification cards you explain casually that you are involved in network marketing, a field it turns out fortuitously, that this person has been considering for several months. One thing leads to another and two weeks later he signs up on your front-line and begins building a huge organization. Do you then spend the rest of your career looking for new imports to back into?"

Everyone laughed, including me. But lost in his humor was a very important fact. There are as many systems as there are successful people in our industry. Some succeed by accident, and others as a result of specific skills. Entrepreneurs are by their very nature innovative, creative, and individualistic. One of the biggest fallacies in MLM is that we should attempt to force creative people to use systems which they don't like and often can't copy.

"People need to prospect a lot of people each week and they need to find a realistic number of legitimate retail customers."

Jeff Piersall's View on Duplication

Jeff Piersall, once a stand-out distributor for Excel, decided to change career directions and become a vice president for Reliv. Jeff is now President of Legacy for Life. Since he's a good friend, I called him to bounce around the idea of duplication. I explained my opinions about the subject but not before asking him to discuss his position on duplication first, so as not to bias him. I didn't want to color his thinking with my own view because he was in such an ideal position to share his own, having succeeded both as a distributor and as a corporate leader. Without any prompting, Jeff laughed and related the truth about his experience in both companies. He said, "You know, when the top nine leaders used to meet to discuss our company, the only thing that we had in common was we had each done our own thing. The biggest complaint was that we just couldn't seem to find people willing to duplicate us! The same thing's true in this company."

My biggest concern about writing a chapter like this is that some might misinterpret my opinions about duplication to mean that we need not give new distributors a track on which to run or any sense of structure. That's not true. New people do need a simple step system as a foundation and encouragement to capitalize on their own strengths and innovation. It is imperative that our recruits understand the tremendous amount of work necessary to succeed in our industry. A few cursory rules are always important. People need to prospect a lot of people each week and they need to find a realistic number of legitimate retail customers. Network marketing, like any other profession, requires a tremendous number of new recruits and to pretend otherwise is preposterous. Finding three or four frontline distributors and working with them exclusively until they succeed would be like an NBA team finding a few college players and ceasing all future recruiting. That team would be a bankrupt franchise within a few seasons. Many networkers fail because they can't manufacture MLM legends out of a handful of average performers.

Why So Much Good Press on Duplication?

Before reviewing what does work better than attempting to get everyone to duplicate one system, I want to say a few words about why the notion of duplication has received so much positive press. There are several reasons in my estimation.

We leaders have an extremely difficult time believing that anyone can succeed without copying our ingenious methods.

Consultants and authors in our industry, many of whom have never actually built any successful downline, have learned that the best way to obtain consulting contracts and speaking engagements is to pander to those leaders who have the mistaken notion that duplication of their brilliance is the only proper way to do this business.

Those who write network marketing books, or have them ghost written by What's His Name, have found that if they glorify duplication, leaders will recommend their books to their downlines.

Duplication involves tremendous profits, especially if leaders demand the purchase of tapes and books which they and their family market to loyal downline members.

I was in a tiny Mexican Village at an open-air vegetable market in the early part of 1995 when I happened upon an amazing scene. Seated on a hand-woven mat in the dusty marketplace was a toothless, seventy-something woman with no shoes and tattered clothing. Next to her on the ground was a battery operated cassette player from which a high-energy, lecture was blasting in Spanish. As her middle aged helper bagged my green onions I inquired about the tape his elderly friend was absorbed in. He informed me that she was a member of a "Tape of The Month Club" in an MLM company and was listening to her most recent audio on how to own your own yacht. He rolled his eyes at me conspiratorially as if we both recognized the nature of the folly.

I suppose there's no such thing as false hope. As long as people dare to dream, anything is possible. But the notion that an impoverished seventy-year old Mexican vegetable vendor could duplicate a thirty-five year old New York lawyer, ultimately owning her own yacht, presumably on a pond somewhere in central Mexico, seemed to me the ultimate example of the absurdity of duplication.

"Your best year in network marketing can begin today with the simple decision to encourage the unique talents of others."

Innovative Encouragement

So, what's the alternative to duplication? It's innovative encouragement. The key is to help new distributors figure out how best to use their own talents to find retail customers and recruit new distributors. An introvert should not be expected to make thirty face-to-face cold calls a day at a local mall. Neither should an extrovert be encouraged to sit alone using direct mail or web page ads to attract a large downline. Whatever you determine to be a person's personal resources, encourage him or her to exploit them.

My number one distributor was Dr. Roy Blizzard. Not only is Roy a tremendous educator, but he is also a much sought-after television talk show guest. His ability to appear on national television and discuss a home business in front of five million viewers is hardly something that can be easily duplicated as a recruiting strategy. Yet, when he did just that; he received letters from 5,000 prospects and five percent of them eventually got involved. Several of those prospects went on to become legends in our industry by exploiting their own talents, yet not one of them has ever duplicated Dr. Blizzard's TV appearances.

Your best year in network marketing can begin today with the simple decision to encourage the unique talents of others. While it may be true that imitation is the highest form of flattery it's not usually the most profitable of activities. And if it's adulation and praise you most crave, rest assured that those in your downline, once wealthy, will pretend that you led them to success even if you didn't. That's the beauty of MLM – just like professional athletics, the team does all the work and the coach gets a ring too!

SUMMARY

Network marketing is not like buying into a franchise. There is not one specific system or technique that everyone duplicates to achieve success in this business. However, this is not to say there are no parameters or guidelines to follow that greatly increase the chance of success. But there are some facts that usually apply:

- Every real network marketing leader has his or her own system for building a downline.

- There is no one person who builds a substantial downline; it is done as a team effort.

- No one ever really duplicates anyone else. We all have our unique attributes, talents, and personalities that influence how we engage in this business.

- It's entrepreneurial innovation, not organizational duplication that works.

- Duplication gets a lot a good press and support from MLM companies because authors and MLM "experts" sell more books and tapes if you think you need to duplicate their methods.

- The secret to network marketing success involves innovative encouragement. In other words, encourage your downline to develop their own method of finding recruits and retail customers.

- Decide now that you will encourage the unique talents of others on your team.

CHAPTER THREE

Prospect List

"Tabula rosa – you begin with a clean slate."

THIS SENTENCE BEGINS YOUR FIRST ACTION DAY IN PROFESSIONAL NETWORKING, whether you just joined a company or you've been with the same one for twenty years. I studied philosophy for a year in college, and one concept stuck: tabula rosa. This means a blank writing tablet. Or you might say, clean slate. I want you to begin with a clean slate. For the next twelve months, you are going to follow this book as your guide and source of inspiration.

If you are unwilling or unprepared to make that personal commitment, put this book down right now and pick it up when you're out of denial. This is not a book from which you might extract little snippets here and there and expect to sail to wealth. To give it a fair shot, you've got to pretend that you're a brand new student of a subject about which you know nothing. Otherwise, you will mentally argue with concepts you think you already understand and select another approach because you happen to feel comfortable applying them. So, here we go: ***tabula rosa***.

Your Prospect List

You probably won't believe this at first, but you know 2,000 people personally. Now obviously I don't mean you know these people like you would your best friend. And you probably can't remember them right now, at least not clearly. But their faces and names are tucked away securely in your mind, just like the words to your favorite ten songs when you were seventeen. You probably can't name ten songs from any year in your adolescence, but you could sing along with every word (or most of the words) of one of those songs if it popped up on a radio. The opening melody (the first three lines) is simply a triggering device.

Your brain sorts people into categories from which you need triggering cues to extract them. Names create faces and faces create names. A telephone book triggers faces as you sort through various names and an old yearbook reverses that process as you look at the faces. I could actually give you a stack of pictures of people you haven't seen in twenty or thirty years and their names would magically pop up from your memory storage. All you really need to help trigger the memory of 2,000 friends, acquaintances, and family is three items: a telephone book, a yearbook and (an) album(s) of vacations. Each time you see a new name, face or job, memories of people you think you've forgotten will come to the surface. To help you in this effort, I've included a memory jogger at the end of this chapter. It's the same, effective memory jogger used by writers in many summaries of great books.

When you finish this chapter, you're going to either use the memory jogger or go get those three sources I mentioned and begin a data base reconstruction of everyone you've ever known or at least been in contact with. You're not going to worry about what you're going to say to these prospects. You're not going to skip that step and rush ahead to see if you can glean new ideas from other chapters. You're not going to roll your eyes and come up with ten brilliant excuses for avoiding those family members and friends.

Look in the mirror and tell yourself eyeball to eyeball that you are earning as much as your family deserves. Can you do that, honestly? If not, get to work on your list.

Excuses, Excuses, Excuses

I've heard all the excuses. They're simply rationalizations. Here are some of them, and hopefully you won't use any of them to prevent yourself from achieving the success you can have:

- Some veterans of ten deals tell me that they simply can't go back to their warm market again.

- Real clueless folks claim they don't even have a warm market.

- Some people have moved recently and insist there is no one they can tap into.

- Some people just feel better about starting with people they don't know.

- Many people believe that a lead generation system of MLM junkies is better than people they personally know, and so on.

I've heard them all and not one excuse is valid. Perhaps the worst is that an individual's friends and family can't possibly or wouldn't possibly do this business. Many people, approached properly, can and will become professional networkers if the company is legitimate and the product is effective. At the very least, they can and will become good customers. And that is a very good thing. Because the fact is, if no one buys the product, there won't be an opportunity to promote.

Who To Contact

Some of you have heard this analogy before, but it needs to be repeated. Were you to stumble into an obscure gold mine and discover five pound nuggets in every wall, you'd probably begin extracting them. If you were to then discover that there were more valuable nuggets than you could possibly ever carry away from the mine, what would you do? Would you run an ad in some MLM publication and invite total strangers to meet you at the mine? Would you buy a list of names, and begin looking for assistant miners? Of course not. You would immediately contact the people you most love and respect.

And you also wouldn't say, "Gee, Fred, I've found a cave and I called to see if you'd consider flying a thousand miles next weekend to explore it with me. I realize we haven't talked in twenty years, but when I found this hole in the ground I thought of you."

When To Move On

Most people treat professional networking like some meaningless hole in the ground rather than the gold mine that it actually is. Then they refuse to call friends or business associates, or if they do, they act almost apologetic for the imposition. If you do not believe that your opportunity is a veritable gold mine, or you are embarrassed to contact your closest and most distant friends, you're not sold on the business. You need to contact someone in your upline immediately and ask them to help you reinvigorate your passion about your opportunity. If no one can sell you on the gold mine you've discovered, and if you truly don't consider it a gold mine, move on. That's critical.

The reason some people never succeed in our profession is because they think from the very outset that they've chosen to participate in a scam. They don't believe they are in early enough, or the product isn't unique, or they don't trust the owners, or the comp plan is impossible to understand. Simply put, if you feel intuitively that you're involved in a hole instead of a gold mine – get out right now and find an opportunity about which you can become passionate.

If more people would simply follow their intuition and refuse to participate in any of the front-end money games emerging everyday in our industry, the scams would dry-up. Too many decent people are willing to gamble in pyramid schemes and that's why scams flourish. I'll tell you more about that later. Remember that just because the circus comes to town, you don't have to ride the elephant.

Compile Your Personal Database

It should take you a minimum of a month from today to compile and approach your personal database. Once you've found your gold mine of unlimited resources, those you've ignored for any reason will resent you for the rest of your life. I'm referring to those who don't eventually become involved in your company and are in someone else's organization. The only thing worse than going to a high school reunion and dealing with the resentment of those whom you refused to contact are those who are earning more than you in another organization of some stranger who got them involved in your own company.

I could write ten more pages on the value of your warm market, but there's no point to it. When I got started in this business, this is what I did. And there are many others who have succeeded beyond the dreams of most, who did exactly same thing. They sat and thought, "Who should I contact about this unique opportunity? I know the product is outstanding, I use it myself. And I want others not only to use the product, but to benefit from the income they can derive in making this product and this opportunity available to others."

So, they sat down and started making a list of names. From this thinking, the 2,000 name list developed.

It's time to take action, stop reading for awhile and make your list. You have to start somewhere, and this is where you start.

Warm Market Memory Jogger

Using these lists, compile your list of 2,000 people you know.

Who Do You Know Who	
Is active in the church You respect Shows genuine concern for other people People always seem to like Does personal counseling (e.g., church leaders, doctors, lawyers, etc.) Is a professional Is in clubs and various group organizations Is active in civic affairs Is in a teaching position in a school/business Deals with the public (e.g., firefighters, mail carriers, city officials, etc.) Is considering a new profession, looking for a job, changing jobs or recently changed jobs, seems to change jobs often Is unable to advance in his/her present job Has talents, but is held back Has just started selling or is an experienced direct sales person Relies on his/ her ideas for livelihood (e.g., author, designer, promoter, advertiser, etc.) Has never been able to get started or has failed in business, but still has strong desires Runs the spa You see at the coffee shop Did your home repairs Is concerned about the condition of their health Is concerned about his/her weight Is in a competitive sport Studies martial arts	Is in a management, supervisory, consultant, trainer capacity Is looking for more out of life Is ambitious, assertive and "on the go" Is considered a leader Attracts leaders Has children just starting junior high, high school or college Has children with special talents that should be developed Wants to set a good example for his/her children to follow Wants to spend more time with his/her family Owns his/her own business Holds a very responsible position that is causing stress/pressure on her Wants to have freedom Is going to college, business or trade school, etc., or has just graduated Was recently married and is just "starting over" Knows everyone in town Has international connections Exudes credibility Is elected to office Works with you now You see at the gym, is into sports, fitness You play sports from your old neighborhood Appraised your home Takes care of your car Is on your Christmas card list You take your dry cleaning to Is your accountant Does your hair Has joint problems Has high cholesterol Needs greater energy

Who Do You Know Who

Are relatives...	Is your...	Sold your...
sisters	mail carrier	house
brothers	insurance agent	shoes
aunts	paper delivery person	car/tires
uncles	(adults)	carpets
children	accountant	TV/stereo
step-relations	dentist	bicycles
cousins	physician	hunting license
parents	minister	camper
grandparents	financial	clothes
	advisor	sports equipment
	lawyer	furniture
	pharmacist	wedding rings
	veterinarian	motorcycle
	optometrist	vacuum cleaner
	florist	boat
		lawn mower
		hunting license
		business cards
		Avon products
		air conditioner
		glasses/contact lenses
		luggage
		kitchen appliances
		Tupperware
		computer
		vitamins

Do You Know Someone Who

Lives next door/across the street
Is your partner's barber/hairdresser
Teaches your children at school
Is the finance director at school
Is president of the PTA
Was your spouse's college fraternity brother/sister
Is your spouse's old high school teacher/principal
Is your child's kindergarten teacher
Was best man/maid of honor/brides-maids/user
Is the purchasing agent where you work
Is your baby-sitter's parent
Goes hunting/fishing with you
Was your military buddy
Painted your house
Owns a drapery business
Manages a tanning salon
Is a deacon in your church
Is in your garden club, book club
Hung your wallpaper
Works with a pest exterminator com-pany
Taught your child "Driver's Ed." this summer

Is the architect who drew your house plans
Are the people you met camping
Is the credit manager of the store where you shop
Repaired your TV
Upholstered your couch
Are people you knew on your old jobs
Went with you to the races
Goes bowling with you
Is a person in your car pool
Installed your telephone
Has a laundromat
Teaches ceramics
Owns a taxi service
Cuts your grass (adults)
Installed your refrigerator
Renewed your driver's license
Is in Rotary/Lions/Kiwanis with you
Is Jaycee president
Delivers parcel post packages
Does your income tax
Plays bridge with you
Sells you gasoline and services your car
Gave you a speeding/parking ticket

Is a...		
Nurse	Welder	Seamstress
Golf pro	Crane operator	Carpenter
Student	Candy salesman	Pilot/flight attendant
Fashion model	Police detective	Motor home dealer
Security guard	Music teacher	Bank cashier/teller
Sheriff	Art instructor	Cloth cutter
Fire chief	Typesetter	Garage mechanic
Secretary	Forester	Editor
Graphic artist	Restaurant owner	Lab technician
Baseball player	Mechanic	Dietician
Anesthetist	Bulldozer operator	Social worker
Surgeon	Bus driver	Lifeguard
Librarian	Airline ticket agent	Race car driver
Mortician	Computer programmer	Paper mill worker
Missionary	Business machine sales-	Brick mason
Real estate agent	person	Drafting manager
Railroad ticket agent	Soft drink distributor	Printer
Newspaper journalist	Air traffic controller	Office manager
Swimming instructor	Interior decorator	Bakery owner
Grocery store owner	Engineer	Disc Jockey
Insurance adjuster	Research technician	Actor/actress
Warehouse manager	Telephone lineman	Land clearer
Moving van operator	Lithographer	Horse trader
Rent-a-car representa-	Fisherman	Statistician
tive	Bench machinist	Cement finisher
TV announcer/pro-	Waitress	Antique dealer
ducer	Furniture dealer	Brewery salesperson
Tool and die maker	Podiatrist	Building contractor
Cookware salesperson	Psychologist	Chiropractor
Dance instructor	Auctioneer	Consultant
Sawmill operator	Electrician	Trainer
Show repairman	Dental hygienist	Horse Trainer
Physical therapist	Professional in baseball/	
Motel owner/manager	basketball/football/	
Highway patrol officer	hockey/tennis/ golf	
Judge		
Academic lecturer		

SUMMARY

Tabula rosa means that you must be prepared to start from scratch to experience your best year in network marketing. But before that you must be completely sold on the company and the product you have chosen to represent.

Also, try to avoid looking for excuses not to proceed with your first most important task-developing a list of warm prospects. To develop your list of warm prospects you must:

- Jog your memory to recall people you know by looking through your highschool yearbook

- Search through your vacation albums and recall people you know from past vacations. Look at photos and take notes of people you recognize.

- Leaf through various names in the telephone book. This does not mean necessarily you will be finding the exact name of someone you know (or an acquaintance), but any given name can jog a name from the past, or a name you simply have not thought about for some time, perhaps for years.

- Use the memory jogger I've supplied to recall names from the past.

CHAPTER FOUR

The Right Tools

*"With the right know-how and equipment,
you can make anything work."*

IF YOU ARE FOLLOWING THE PROCESS CORRECTLY, you now have a goal (or several goals) that demands more money than you personally need, and you have a list of several hundred prospects. If that's not the case, you've skipped ahead and begun a new chapter without completing the first steps. The reason such a small percentage of people ever earn the big money in our industry is that they resist accepting guidance from those who have succeeded. They look for shortcuts, for the easy way. It's not too late to go back to the first three chapters and take those steps I've suggested. Please do so if you haven't already.

*"Regardless of how shy or inexperienced you
may be, success is possible in MLM if you hand
out the right tools to large numbers of people."*

Professional Material

In this brief chapter, we'll examine the tools you need to successfully prospect your warm market and filter through them to find those ready for what you have to offer. You should have at least two of the following recruiting/retailing/filtering tools:

- an audio tape
- fax-on-demand
- web site
- brochure
- recorded conference call on a web site
- dedicated telephone line
- a video and/or a CD
- recorded conference call on telephone line

No matter how eloquent you may be, professional sales tools which are provocative and informative work when personal dialogue does not. They have a dual purpose. First, they provide information and excitement, and second, they serve to help you quickly sift through and find the right people.

Regardless of how shy or inexperienced you may be, success is possible in MLM if you hand out the right tools to large numbers of people. Sales tools are the great equalizer in our industry. I've seen maids achieve millionaire status and mayors fail miserably all because they followed or ignored this concept. No matter how articulate, few networkers convince friends to change careers by attempting to persuade them to do so without proper tools that serve as a source of credibility and verification.

One of the most amazing facts about MLM is that many companies have become multi-million dollar dynasties without substantive products, adequate capital or ethical leaders. How did they do that? They prospered because they had extremely persuasive tools which convinced people to make emotional, uninformed decisions.

Some industry outsiders marvel about the fact that it's possible for a little company with nothing but a mediocre long distance service or me-too type of supplement to build 300 million dollar revenues on the strength of one particularly good audio or video recruiting tool. Others are impressed that new life can be breathed into a nearly dead company by the simple creation of an effective recruiting or product tool.

One industry leader, Curt Wilkins, called me recently and shared a graphic example of what happened in his own company based on this concept of using the right tools. I think his example, like so many others I've heard over the years, quite eloquently supports my point. He was kind enough to draft the experience and send it to me to include in this book.

The Wilkins' Story

"Kathy and I joined MLM in April of 1990. For the prior 25 plus years, I had been a successful real estate broker in Boise, Idaho. We quickly achieved various ranks and were honored to be inducted into the prestigious President's Club.

"Initially Kathy and I were less than enthusiastic about the image of the MLM industry as a whole. We had previously signed up in two network marketing companies, but had really not pursued those opportunities. But, with one company, we witnessed life-changing product experiences, both personally and with family members and decided with this valid product and an extremely strong company, we could proceed with promoting the opportunity without reservations.

"Unfortunately, the quality of the promotional materials produced by the company at that time did not have the quality of content we needed. Often company-produced materials lack the sizzle that distributor-produced materials offer. After hearing Mark Yarnell's concept of creating your own recruiting tools, we contacted the President of Blue Ribbon Video, Lance Blair, and shared our idea for a new video. We offered to do the scripting and acting, provided he would cover the production costs. We negotiated for Blue Ribbon to keep all profits, and they marketed the videos and audios for us. It was a win-win situation for everybody. In 18 months, over 1.5 million copies of our materials had sold through Blue Ribbon.

> *"Those organizations that continue to prosper decade after decade are led by individuals in the field who are constantly re-inventing the opportunity."*

"Kathy and I produced the video sitting in a living room with a fireplace in the background. We looked directly into the camera and talked as though each prospect was sitting in our living room with us. We talked to them personally. It was a huge success and it worked beyond our wildest dreams. We had calls from all over the United States thanking us for a video that they could simply 'plug and play' in their own homes. Pay attention to the advice Mark Yarnell offers. His suggestions enabled us to earn over $625,000 in the 5 years we were involved with Nikken."

Old Company/New Tools

The importance of an effective recruiting/retailing tool cannot be overstated. It's especially critical to the person involved in an old and stable company or a brand new company. A casual stroll through the history of our industry proves my point. Those organizations that continue to prosper decade after decade are led by individuals in the field who are constantly re-inventing the opportunity. Every few years a new division emerges with brand new starter kits and new recruiting tools are initiated by the field leaders. It's what I call a "new ground floor."

New Ground Floor

The danger is this: If the distributors don't create their own "new ground floor," the corporate team will. And in some cases, a corporate move actually stalls rather than invigorates growth. Until you've been in a company that implements a compensation plan "enhancement" that reduces your check thirty percent, you won't understand. So let me make it very simple. If leaders don't exercise their personal rights and responsibilities as independent distributors, corporate folks will attempt to control the field. And I have observed that most of their attempts are counter-productive.

Some corporate leaders may decide to lead your company into a merger or sell-out. Others might actually create a huge number of less than provocative sales tools. Some companies change comp plans for the worse and others bring in outside consultants who are ridiculously incompetent. All this because their top leaders have become too lazy to reinvent the field themselves.

I've seen this problem occur dozens of times because unless a company is growing, the corporate leaders have no basis of self-validation. Growth is all that matters to many corporations. They care neither how profitable the company might be nor how comfortable the distributors might be; growth is the corporate report card. So the field must create new sales tools and new ground floor opportunities or the company will attempt to do so. Those same upline leaders who initially drove the company to millions in sales have the ability to do the same thing again with new stories, new kits and new recruiting tools.

"Those same upline leaders who initially drove the company to millions in sales have the ability to do the same thing again..."

Those folks in a new company must especially take the initiative to create their own provocative tools or momentum will never occur. Our industry is filled with examples of companies that have become international dynasties by skillfully marketing products or services of dubious value, while others with remarkable products have gone out of business over night. Why? Because of the marketing tools created by the field leaders.

The Power of "The Story"

The Tulip deal in Holland during the 1600s demonstrated the power of "the story." One skillfully developed brochure launched a sales frenzy that eventually caused Tulips to be valued higher than gold or Rembrandt paintings. In the modern world some networking companies have become billion dollar dynasties by the skillful marketing of soap and vitamins, web sites and long distance.

Of course I'm not suggesting that all such examples bode well for our industry. What I am saying is that once you've found a legitimate company with emotional, efficacious and consumable products, the opportunity to prosper is unlimited provided you've got good recruiting tools. So whether you've joined an upstart or a twenty-year-old company, you'll need effective prospecting tools. Anyone with a little imagination can create a great set of tools. Here's how it's done.

Making The Greatest Set of Tools

Pick the greatest selling points about your products and opportunity and draft a script for an audio, web site and brochure. It helps to find a set of tools that has worked for other companies in the past and follow their format. Study great audio tapes and videos. The recruiting tools should be truthful and emotional. They may include the testimonials of distributors who have gone from rags to riches in a short time or product testimonials from customers who have benefited dramatically from your product line. It doesn't take a slick, skillful sales person to create sales tools. In fact, the more down-to-earth and believable the distributor, the more effective will be the tool.

There are two things critical about these kinds of recruiting tools. First, they should be offered to your organization at your cost. Your goal must be to avoid regulatory problems while earning tremendous income through the legitimate movement of company products to end consumers. You might be tempted to profit from sales tools, but that's the dinosaur approach.

The big money in today's networking arena results from product movement and not from the movement of sales aids. In the old days of MLM, leaders would consistently earn more money from tapes, books, and brochures than the actual movement of company products. That was fair and it still is. It's called free enterprise. But in today's world everyone knows that an audio can be dubbed for a quarter and many folks consider it offensive that their uplines would sell a tape for ten times that amount. It's not unethical or immoral. It's simply stupid and greedy.

It's important to keep in mind that the essence of network marketing has always been the process of recruiting a large organization to move a significant amount of products or services to the largest possible number of people. Those leaders who figure out the best and most inexpensive way for folks to do that, will ultimately achieve the most wealth. Some would argue that any leader who creates a great tool deserves to profit dramatically. I agree. It's a question of whether that leader feels better about profiting from his organization's success or at their expense. Either your people will appreciate your efforts to provide them with low-cost tools, or they will resent your willingness to profit from their sales and purchases.

It's also very important to keep this simple concept in mind; a leader is someone who demonstrates what is possible. If your actions imply that the way to prosper in MLM is to create sales tool profits through exorbitant pricing, that's what your people will plan to do. Pretty soon, all your best people will be focused on generating side money rather than product movement. There are some phenomenal distributors in MLM who have left our industry in order to pursue a career in lead generation systems, recruiting tools and consulting. That's everyone's loss. No one ends up sadder than the dynasty builder who has lost the vision of passive residual income.

Create Some Excitement

So let's assume that you are in a new company or an old one that needs some excitement. Take a few days to put together some exciting facts about your opportunity and products. The more dramatic they are, the better so long as the facts are accurate. Write a simple script that can be recorded on audio and/or drafted into a brochure. Submit it to your company's legal department for approval. Once approved, book a couple of hours at a local recording studio in order to record your tape. Find a duplication company willing to dub it in large quantities for twenty-five or thirty cents. Record the tape, get it copied, then begin circulating the recruiting /retailing tool to all your leaders.

Those who are skilled in web site design may want to create a recruiting site with similar information. Many MLM companies offer self-replicating web sites to all distributors so you may want to use one of those.

The main thing to remember is that anyone can invent or reinvent a ground floor opportunity regardless of their skills or background. In my own case, with zero experience in MLM or tape sales, I created an audio in 1987 called "Rags To Riches." It sold over a million copies and my income from skin care products grew to over $30,000 a month. My company experienced huge growth from that one simple tool, yet, I never earned one penny in royalties. The $33,000 a month income from the networking business was more than adequate.

In September 2000, I joined a new company and created a brand new audio that is, at the time of this writing, selling over 300,000 copies a month. Just prior to September, I spoke to a 40 year old MLM company at their annual convention and one of their distributors decided to create a new ground floor opportunity. She followed the advice I just gave you and her downline is absolutely exploding as a result.

Remember, you are an independent distributor in a wonderful profession in which no one other than you can impose limits on yourself. There are no rules beyond integrity and common sense. No one can stop you from creating your own tools and growing your own business. You don't have to be a professional recording genius to create and duplicate a powerful recruiting tool. You don't have to be an expert at public relations to draft and produce an emotional brochure. All you need are courage and conviction. In the next chapter we'll explore the importance of numbers now that you've got goals, names, and tools ready to go.

SUMMARY

All professionals have tools of some type to use in their work. As a professional network marketer, you definitely need sales and recruiting tools. Here are some important points to consider:

- You do not need to be eloquent to succeed in network marketing, you just need the right tools.

- Sales tools help you demonstrate the effectiveness of your product.

- Recruiting tools help you turn a retail customer into a networker in your downline.

- Sales and recruiting tools are critical to jumpstart a new company, and to reinvigorate an old, established company.

- If you don't create sales tools, the corporate executives of your company will, but their tools will probably be inferior to yours.

- To create sales/recruiting tools, you don't have to be a marketing expert, you just need to be down-to-earth, tell inspiring stories, provide compelling testimonials, and list all the positive aspects of your product and company.

- Create any of a variety of tools including audio tapes, videos, a website, or a brochure.

- Don't try to make a profit on your sales tools; give them away, or make them available at close to your cost.

CHAPTER FIVE

Numbers, Numbers, Numbers

"There are no lucky shortcuts because MLM, like all other sales, is based solely on numbers."

SOME OF YOU HAVE NOW PREPARED YOURSELF FOR YOUR BEST YEAR in network marketing. You have set meaningful goals that you are passionate about, you have a substantial database of warm prospects, and you have the sales tools necessary to approach them.

The only remaining task before actually kick-starting your business is critical: pick a number between one and fifty. Now this is not an arbitrary number. This is a very specific number that will represent the amount of prospects you honestly intend to contact on a daily basis for the next year, and preferably for the rest of your life. Make certain that the number you select is realistic given your other commitments, responsibilities and the number of hours you can actually work on your MLM business.

I recommend that when you sit down to get going, you attempt to contact four people per hour. You do this because a significant percentage of folks will not be reachable in any given hour, on any given day. And keep in mind, the number you select should reflect those prospects you actually intend to contact rather than just "attempt" to contact. Which means, after an initial call, and they are not there, keep calling until you reach someone.

Pick A Number

This number is critical. When I first started in networking, my initial goal was five contacts per hour for six hours a day, five days a week. My mentor told me that if I approached thirty people a day I would actually sign up 5% or one a day based on a twenty-day month. He was absolutely right.

Although that number of daily contacts was hugely ambitious, I will always appreciate Richard Kall for setting the bar so high. During my first half year I signed up 189 front line and my monthly income surpassed $15,000, which in 1986, was a fortune to me. Today that number of contacts seems to scare folks, but it was simple – and still is. Part of the reason it's easy is the simplicity of the approach which we will discuss at length in the next chapter. There's nothing complicated about a one – sentence question.

"The more people you approach, the more people will sign up as distributors."

Above all else remember this: sales of any kind are strictly a "numbers game." The more people you approach, the more people will sign up as distributors. The more personally sponsored distributors, the larger your group. The larger the group, the greater your sales. The more you earn, the more people sign up. And the cycle continues to repeat itself. Anyone who preaches otherwise is wrong. Period. End of the story. There are no lucky short cuts because MLM, like all other sales, is based solely on numbers.

A.L. Williams

To this date, the best materials I've ever reviewed on network marketing are the books and tapes of A.L. Williams. When people ask me to recommend a book, I always suggest that they order a copy of Williams' classic *All You Can Do Is All You Can DO But*

All You Can Do Is Enough! It's certainly more important than any book I've written. His audios, if you can find copies, are wonderfully informative and motivational. During one of his lectures to his own field distributors he gave an example that has remained forever emblazoned in my mind. I probably won't do his example justice, but here's what I remember about it.

During the mid-fifties, W. Clement Stone, co-founder of *Success* magazine and CEO of Combined Insurance Company, was retained to train a group of insurance sales people in Chicago where sales were dismal. The sales force was averaging one sale a week per agent and the district manager was unable to help them achieve higher numbers. According to Stone, after interviewing half the agents, he determined that the agents were easily capable of selling one policy a day by simply changing one element of their work schedule: their number of approaches.

To prove his point, Stone created the most absurd recruiting question conceivable. The district manager argued that it would never work. Stone taught each salesperson to knock on a stranger's door and ask a simple question: "You don't want to buy any insurance do you?" His strategy, in the form of a contest, was to determine exactly how many prospects each agent would have to approach in order to obtain one sale.

Everyone in the company was convinced that no one would even sell a single policy. But they made an amazing discovery. When any sales person knocked on sixty doors with the same question, one prospect would respond affirmatively. Eventually someone would say; "Well, actually we are in the market for insurance and were just talking about it." Once Stone was able to demonstrate that simple approach, it then became simply a matter of making sixty approaches a day to make one sale. In a very short time each agent was averaging five sales a week and once the approach was refined, that number grew to eight per week. Why? Because sales have always been about numbers.

Finding 30 People Per Day

You could say nearly anything about MLM to thirty strangers a day and sign up one of them. I learned that lesson by cold calling people in Austin, Texas. As I stated earlier, my mentor told me that to succeed in networking I needed to sign up one person a day for six months and that all I needed to do was approach thirty a day. He was right. Ultimately that group, created my first six months, expanded my efforts and resulted in over ten million dollars income.

So the next step is to pick a number between one and fifty. That number will represent precisely how many folks you intend to prospect each day. Remember that each approach will last no more than two minutes. In the next chapter, you'll learn the very best words to use in your approach.

There are two facts about MLM which must be remembered by distributors who are truly eager to earn the big checks. The first is that there are plenty of prospects anywhere in the world at any given time. It is impossible to avoid bumping into thirty people a day unless you are chained to a tree in the wilderness. I've been amazed by the number of folks who ask me how in the world I find thirty people a day to approach. I don't get it. Last year a hiker was lost in a snowstorm up in the mountains by Lake Tahoe. Eventually, hundreds of people joined the search and by the second day a search team of nine rescue workers found him holed up in an old abandoned shack halfway up a mountain. I thought to myself: "Isn't that interesting, even a lost hiker has nine prospects come to him in under forty-eight hours."

Gas Stations & Audio Tapes

I can't pump my own gas at any gas station without giving audio tapes to at least four people. One day a guy in San Francisco was complaining about no leads and I took him into a grocery store and we counted seventy-one people in five minutes. Next we walked into a bookstore and in less than half an hour twenty prospects walked up to the business book section. We noticed that four of them were interested in a home-based business by merely observing which specific books they picked up. There are thousands of people wandering around in every location in North America, Europe and Asia, and an estimated forty percent of them will change jobs within four years. Don't ever delude yourself into thinking that you can't find people to approach.

Prospect For Life

The second fact is that every prospect is a prospect for life. Each time you approach a person one more time, your odds of recruiting him or her will increase dramatically. That's true for two reasons. First, each time you approach a person your income has risen dramatically since the last time. Second, each time you approach a person the odds that she is about to change jobs also increase. Thus it is important to keep a file of contacts and contact each person every six months until they either sign up on your frontline or die.

One final thought: don't lie to yourself. Whether you decide to prospect ten people a day or fifty – do it. If you insist on conning your sponsor into believing that you are actually working, that's up to you. But don't con yourself. I am shocked by the number of people who blame their failure in MLM on everyone and everything except their own inactivity. When a distributor in my organization tries to persuade me that he's talking to thirty people a day five days a week and has only signed up two people in a month, I call BS. Because even if a person is saying everything wrong, but saying it enough times, and with sincerity, success is inevitable.

What's Your Lucky Number?

Remember, in MLM success is sifting through numbers, numbers, numbers. In the next chapter, we'll examine the very best approach possible so that you can maximize your effectiveness. But right now, before moving on, make a solid commitment and write it down:

"Each day, without exception, I will contact

_____ people."

SUMMARY

MLM is a numbers game. Many people are looking for an easy way to make the big dollars in network marketing. But there is no easy way. This business requires effort. And you can either be serious and proceed with serious intent, or you'll never achieve the money and success you fantasize about. Here are the points to consider:

- Great tools actually recruit people, but also act as a filter.

- Pick a number that represents the number of people you actually contact every day to tell them about your product and the opportunity you're excited about.

- Be realistic about the number you pick. Make sure the number is a number you will actually do.

- As you start to make your calls, try to reach four people an hour.

- Determine in advance how many hours you can realistically commit to contacting people.

- Keep this mantra in mind: "The more people I approach, the more people I will sign up as distributors."

- Don't delude yourself into thinking that you can't find prospects – they're everywhere, at the store, the mall, on the street, everywhere.

- Each prospect is a prospect for life. Circumstances change. When a person says no today, it doesn't mean they will say no in six months.

- There are no short cuts to success in network marketing – it's all about the numbers.

CHAPTER SIX

The Approach

"Approached properly and professionally, most people will take a serious look at MLM."

I'VE READ AND HEARD MULTITUDES OF DIFFERENT prospecting and retailing approaches. There are countless systems, from slow, don't-talk-business, "relationship prospecting," to rapid-fire shotgun questions calculated to provoke interest. Of more significance than what tactics you use is your knowledge of what prospects already believe and your attitude.

Money Equals Success

First, prospects believe that money equals success and big money equals big status and big success. Some cultures believe even more fervently in the illusory nature of money. That's why people in some countries who have been fired have been known to commit suicide. Universally, money has become the adult report card. In fact, it's why we spend our best years in school. In America, we've shifted to an educational system that teaches us how to take tests rather than how to gain knowledge. Why? Because if we pass tests we are promoted to the next level. No one can afford to be left behind even one year because graduation means money. Degrees mean jobs and the better the job the more money we presumably earn.

Rest assured, virtually everyone you will approach is interested in two things:

- big money
- free time

Of course, the emphasis is on big money. Supposedly, the pot at the end of the adult rainbow is called "golden" because that's when we get to do nothing but play and spend money. People want free time because they are convinced that the absence of productivity will be fulfilling. Golf and fishing are supposed to equal prestige and joy.

"The truly successful leaders in MLM earn more at home than cardiac surgeons earn in operating theaters."

In the year 2001, CNN ran a special story that asked the deepest philosophical question of our age: "Does Tiger Woods have more power than Nelson Mandella?" After all, Mandella may have run a country, but he doesn't have the money that Tiger has. Isn't that profound? Don't get me started.

So, proceed from the assumption that every prospect worth recruiting wants big money and free time. The third thing to keep in mind is that by age thirty, most men and women are living in a functional coma from which they may only be awakened by a conscious shock of considerable magnitude. Most folks will remain in dead end jobs working forty to seventy hours a week doing tasks they hate for bosses they detest until they are too old to experience joy. Unless you shock them with a provocative question, they will remain in a daze and continue to pretend that they were put on earth to mindlessly fight traffic six days a week in order to live in subdivisions further and further away from the work they deplore.

Ask the average person any question calculated to force them to consider the futility of their lives and they go into an immediate defense mode. They've usually been lied to by everyone important in their lives for so long that most have memorized rapid responses to provocative questions. Canned responses include: "I'm from

Missouri...," "if it sounds too good to be true..." "that's one of them pyramid schemes..." and on and on.

Shocking Approaches

Only the most shocking approaches will awaken a North American, European or Asian from his mediocrity. Because your best year in network marketing will probably be the year you recruit the most people, you'll need to learn an approach that gets you past the comas. Your approach should be truthful but so provocative that it gets even the most jaded and cynical person's attention. And how do you get their attention?

Talk about money. Of course, that's an easy and provocative thing to bring up because the truly successful leaders in MLM earn more at home than cardiac surgeons earn in operating theaters. More important, skilled networkers enjoy all the free time they desire by working at home. Cardiac surgeons are lucky to get any free time.

Although some networkers are still relying on hotel meetings, most of us have opted for streamlined telephone systems-at home. Indeed, most leaders have come to realize that speaking in public is not particularly effective as a recruiting technique anymore.

What Doesn't Work

Before explaining what really works, let's be candid about what doesn't. Let me begin with describing what I call the parasites of free enterprise.

There have always been parasites in free enterprise. We normally don't call them parasites because that has a negative connotation, but that's precisely what they are.

The fascinating truth about parasites is that sometimes they earn more than those participating in the primary activity. For example, during the gold rush of the last century, the prostitutes and saloon owners frequently earned more than the miners to whom they were catering.

Some of today's MLM parasites are prospering by using impressive high tech online methods to succeed. There are "experts" that no one has ever heard of who post web sites and send newsletters, teach seminars and write books. Online spams, e-zines and unsolicited e-mailings are making vendors wealthy at the expense of unwary distributors by promising success without effort. Not only that, expensive leads are being sold and resold online often with bogus telephone numbers and non-existent web addresses. There are even co-op ads circulating with the names of prospects who aren't really interested in MLM.

Low tech approaches – though no less effective – continue to take advantage of unsuspecting networkers. Some of the culprits include publishers that circulate magazines in which articles of dubious information are printed as long as the author's MLM company is willing to spend thousands on advertising in the magazine. Then there are still plenty of seminars conducted by skilled speakers on how to build a big business although the speaker has never personally built a viable downline. And of course audio tapes and videos flourish and are sold throughout the world disseminating information that only confuses people about our industry or misleads them about what really works to build a successful business.

Big Hitter Frauds

A "big hitter" in MLM was once defined as a person who had earned millions in one company. Today, I hear from self-described "big hitters" who have failed at ten deals and have a database of a thousand MLM junkies who have failed with them. Not a week goes by that some parasite doesn't call me with a great new recruiting or lead generation system. When I ask them to provide the name of one person who is successful as a result of using their new system, they act indignant. Often the pitch ends up with: "You'll be the first! Eventually everyone will be using this new concept." Right.

The Internet Exposed

I realize that some of my opinions will be rejected by those who make their living as parasites. One thing I've learned about being visible and honest is that one becomes an easy target for those whom he's willing to expose. However, once you've been the target of a scorned ex-wife and mediocre competitors, it becomes much easier to tell the truth without fear or concern.

There is a good old boys club in MLM just like in any other business. A large number of MLM parasites work together to promote systems that truly don't work. I could dedicate many pages to the ineffective systems of the past, but the latest one that stands out is this: the Internet. CNN calls it the "misinformation highway."

The Internet is a great tool for providing the world with company and product information. I use our corporate web site many times each day. I also have a great flash presentation. At some point it may become an effective lead acquisition tool, but right now it's a major waste of time for that purpose.

"The most frightening thing about the Internet is that most people have no idea who authors many web sites."

I realize alleged MLM coaches and authors are promoting the Internet as a lead generation tool. So? Does that mean it's working? Would someone please send me the name of one credible authority who has used an Internet lead system that has enabled three or four MLM people to earn $100,000 a month? Or how about providing the name of just one person who has earned that much consistently in one company for just one year through using leads generated from online banner ads or e-zines? Eventually, someone will figure out how to use the Internet effectively, but to date, no one has done so. If I'm wrong, call me and I'll introduce your system in the next

---

reprint of this book. Until then, it's time to stop reading about the Internet "buzz" in MLM as if credible people were really writing about it.

"No one could provide me with evidence of web approach systems that have worked."

And how about those bogus MLM web sites created by self-proclaimed experts? Who are these people who create the mlm.coms? I use Kim Klavor's info because she's a real expert, but where did the others come from and when did they actually build a long-term downline? Who are these "authorities?"

The most frightening thing about the Internet is that most users have no idea who authors many web sites. Does anyone bother to question the credentials of those MLM web masters? I did once. I discovered that the guy was averaging several thousand hits a day, yet had never been involved in actual downline recruiting. Nor had he ever been involved in corporate operations. No wonder half the information on his site was bogus. In fact, the best networkers I've ever met would have failed had they followed this guy's advice. Another one who pretends to be an industry watchdog is a distributor for one company and consistently uses his site to fabricate lies about competitors.

"Success results more often from attitude than ability, but if you don't have either...try another profession."

I know a lot of great people in MLM and while writing this book I called eight major leaders to get their opinions on the Internet as a viable lead generation tool. No one could provide me with evidence of web approach systems that have worked. Several told me that they believe that it's not the Internet systems that are at fault, but rather the kind of prospects one attracts over the Web. They also feel that most web surfers just aren't cut out to succeed in relationship marketing. I believe they may be right.

The Correct Approach

Network marketing by definition is the word-of-mouth distribution of legitimate products to end consumers combined with the professional recruitment and training of additional distributors to further distribute those products. Professional recruitment means just that. Can you imagine Xerox or IBM or some other big company closing their human resources and recruitment offices in favor of fax blasts and Internet banner ads?

Approached properly and professionally most people will take a serious look at MLM. Approached coldly through mass contact systems, few people will entertain the notion of changing careers. Remember, there's no such thing as "virtual passion."

Let's use Internet statistics as an example. According to Red Herring, an expert Internet source, "less than 1% of all banner ads result in any kind of profitable sales to the advertiser." If I were guessing, based on feedback from lots of users of Internet recruiting systems, no system currently available has even produced a consistent income of $50,000 a month in our industry. So why do people keep paying for expensive lists and banner ads? Because they are grossly misinformed. It's one of the many reasons I wrote this book.

The best way to distribute products is to ask people to buy them. If you can't look another human being in the eyes and ask her to buy what you're selling, get out of marketing network or otherwise. If you don't believe so fervently in your product that you are passionate about sharing it with everyone you've ever known, quit marketing or get into a solid company with a meaningful product. If you can't passionately approach ten or fifteen real human beings each day with the opportunity to retire wealthy in a couple of years, get out of MLM. Do not be deluded by MLM parasites into believing that they can give you systems which will allow you to prosper without productive marketing.

You don't have to be beautiful or educated, but you do have to work hard and be extremely passionate about the product and opportunity you are selling or YOU WILL FAIL. Success results more often from attitude than ability, but if you don't have either...try another profession. MLM is a SELLING PROFESSION. It's not a lottery. I would rather talk personally to five people a day than email 500. Most quality entrepreneurs don't even bother to read unsolicited attachments any longer anyway!

Straightforward Selling

The best approach to selling is straightforward. Also, make sure you keep your approach very brief. Then, whether you're talking to a complete stranger or a family friend, and after you got past the usual preliminary niceties (i.e., How are you? I'm fine. Blah, blah, blah.) ask these two things:

- will they buy your product and/or

- will they consider looking at your opportunity.

Everything else is just fluff.

After breaking the ice, I ask people two simple questions this way (and feel free to use my words, verbatim, if you wish):

"If I had a product that could make your life much better and you could afford it, would you buy it from me?"

And:

"If you knew for sure that it was possible to earn $100,000 a month legally and retire in two years, would that be a business you would at least want to know about?"

Remember, before you can proceed with a prospect you need to find out a little bit about their brainpower. You don't ever want to recruit idiots because they're no fun to work with. Any man or woman who doesn't want to purchase a product that will dramatically improve his or her life at a price they can afford is not real bright.

Of course when you use a straightforward, honest approach you will obviously encounter skepticism. After all, in today's world there's usually a catch. People aren't normally straightforward and honest unless there's a hidden agenda. Most prospects will assume that it's a trick question. The only trick is to prove there isn't one. You've got to emphasize that you can verify both the product and price and that if you can they will buy it. And, you've got to be able to demonstrate that it is possible to earn $100,000 a month, but that's easy if you're with a great, legitimate company.

What If You Get A "YES"?

So, let's say you asked these questions of at least 30 people and all of a sudden, someone surprises you and says, "Yes, I am interested." Good heavens, what do you do then? Relax.

Those prospects who express a desire to earn that kind of money and achieve freedom should then be immediately directed to a website, or you provide them with an audio tape, video or a recorded conference call. Those who aren't interested should be politely excused from any further discussion and filed for a later approach. How might this work in a hypothetical conversation? Consider this:

"Well, Nancy, if you're interested in doing a bit of research, let me give you a tape to listen to and check out our website (and you provide the website address). This will probably answer most of your questions."

That's it. Then, a couple days later, you follow this encounter with a follow-up call. Don't get caught up in any discussion about your product, opportunity or company information. Your only objective in the first approach is to point prospects in the right direction so they can gather more information. When they have done their due diligence and get back in contact with you, the next step is to direct them to your upline or sign them up immediately. Don't waste your time arguing, selling or closing prospects. Remember this above all else; MLM is a numbers game until people sign up and then it becomes a "people" game. Your upline will deal with all questions and objections for you until you are proficient. Don't worry about learning the minutiae about your company. You should be able to learn everything you need from your upline's three-way conversations. A three-way is a telephone call during which you, your prospect and your upline are linked simultaneously.

Because you are an independent distributor I respect your right to alter that approach. Many new distributors are afraid to talk about such huge incomes. Others think they are smarter than those of us who have earned millions in MLM. So let me make one simple point: the only relevant system is one that has worked. This one has worked and is working today. So, do what you want.

How Many Times Do You Ask These Questions?

The number of times you ask those two questions each day will dictate the amount of MLM success you will enjoy. If you aren't earning a reasonable income in six months, ask more people to participate. If you aren't selling enough product, ask more people to buy your product.

But whatever you do, don't get sucked into a numbers game parasite strategy that allows you to reach 10,000 people in six hours. They do not work. Period. End of story. They are just like hotel meetings. The reason some leaders insist on doing them is because they don't work. If they did work, they'd be obsolete in four meetings. Think about it; if one hundred guests each brought five prospects to the weekly meeting four weeks in a row, which hotel in your town has a ballroom that will accommodate 21,600 people? While hotel meetings are designed to pad the egos of leaders who love to speak, most lead generation systems are sold to line the pockets of MLM parasites who have not built a downline.

Instead, they make money from audio tapes, videos, books, and speaking fees.

So, practice your simple questions.

What If Your Prospect Is Still Interested?

Let's go back to our prospect, Nancy. You call her back a couple days later and she amazes you by saying that she is actually interested in your product and the opportunity. Now what?

Again, keep things simple. At this time you tell Nancy you want to schedule a three-way conference call between you, her, and your upline partner. Presumably, Nancy has heard the tape or watched the informative video, and possibly studied the information available at the company website. This ensures that your upline partner does not have to spend a whole lot of extra time just explaining the basics.

Now, during the course of the conference call, just let your partner do the closing. Let them field questions and prepare your prospect for becoming a new distributor. Remember, the inherent value of upline support stems from the knowledge of your leaders. Someone, somewhere in your upline, is earning a great deal of money and has a vested interest in your success. By listening closely to the manner in which your upline answers your prospect, you can learn how to perform similar three-ways for your people. The three-way is an ideal prospecting and training tool.

On the assumption that everything has gone well, after the three-way conference call, it is now appropriate to ask Nancy if she is ready to sign up. After you have signed up your new distributor, take the time to teach them how to go out and pursue prospects.

Above all else, remember this: Don't let new distributors complicate this process. Many, left alone, will delve into minutiae and remain there until they fail. By following this system I've created two million-dollar-plus annual incomes in my ventures.

Networkers Vs. The Company

There are countless recruiting systems out there but nothing beats a simple, honest approach. If companies ever figure out how to successfully build sales and huge organizations with systems instead of distributors, networkers will be out of business and companies will be 58% more profitable by cutting out override checks.

"If companies ever figure out how to successfully build sales and huge organizations with systems instead of distributors, networkers will be out of business and companies will be 58% more profitable by cutting out override checks."

If you don't understand this, think about the implications for about an hour and then you'll start prospecting people.

SIX STEP RECRUITING PROCESS

Here is a brief overview of the prospecting/signing up process:

1. Create a database of prospects from any and all sources.

2. Call or speak to each person in this database, and ask them the big money and free time questions.

3. Direct any interested prospects to your sales tools – audio tape, video, voice message, website, brochure, whatever.

4. Contact interested prospects a couple of days later to learn if they are still interested. If so, arrange for a three-way call between you, your prospect, and your upline partner.

5. After the three-way, ask if your prospect is ready to sign-up as a distributor.

6. Train your new distributor to follow this system and approach.

SUMMARY

The approach to network marketing is the one thing so many people seem to want to avoid. It's as if they want to sell without having to sell. But that's not how it works. Here are some points to keep in mind with respect to approaching prospects when introducing your product and opportunity:

- Big money and more free time are the two main reasons why anyone would take an interest in network marketing.

- Don't think that shortcuts work when approaching prospects. They simply don't work.

- Avoid the MLM parasites who promise a quick and easy way to success in network marketing-all you have to do is buy their audio tape, video, book, or attend their expensive lecture. Read my lips: "Just say no."

- Forget the Internet as a means to attract prospects until someone starts earning big money using them instead of just selling them. Banner ads, e-zines, e-blasts, etc. are still unproven.

- Use the Internet to gather and provide information only. Your MLM company probably has a website. Check it out to make sure you know about your product, any corporate developments, etc. Consider your own flash presentation.

- Straightforward selling is the most effective way to approach prospects and get them to either purchase the product or become involved in the opportunity you impart to them.

- There are two straightforward questions to ask a prospect. In their simplest form, those questions are:

- will they buy your product and/or

- will they consider looking at your opportunity

- The fact is, the more people you approach and ask these questions, the more distributors you will sign up.

CHAPTER SEVEN

Partnering

"Common sense told me there was some person above me who was smarter, wealthier and more compatible with me than my sponsor."

BY NOW YOU'VE PROBABLY GROWN WEARY OF MY INSISTENCE at the beginning of each chapter that you should have already taken the steps suggested in each previous chapter. I have a reason. Few people ever perform the necessary steps to really succeed in network marketing. Those people who will be earning big money in under a year have followed my advice thus far. Of those who are telling themselves that after reading these chapters they will then go back and take action, few will. This is not a bedtime story. If you haven't acted on my suggestions, stop reading right now and begin again, because this chapter is critical, but will not be of value until you've done everything else. Selecting a partner will not help you until you can prepare your partner for exactly what you expect of him or her.

Everyone in every great company, with the exception of the Master Distributor, has wonderful people with whom to partner. I could never have earned so many millions of dollars in my former

MLM company had I not figured out the need for a partner (better known as a mentor).

Common sense told me two things: first, there was some person above me who was smarter, wealthier and more compatible with me than my sponsor. Second, that person had a financial stake in my success. So, I literally began calling everyone in my upline until I found Richard Kall. The rest is history.

Sponsor Ethics

It's critical to sign up directly under the first person who introduces you to an opportunity. I know of zero exceptions to that rule. Sponsor shopping is like eating at a Mexican restaurant and walking next door and paying the bill at a Chinese restaurant. A culture of ethics in every company is critical. When distributors have to worry about losing prospects whom they have recruited or spent considerable time courting into their business, that company is destined for trouble. I've heard all the excuses for signing up under people other than those who introduced prospects to the company. None of them makes sense.

We may receive ten packets about one company, but someone had to have sent the first one. The person who introduced us may be incompetent but that is irrelevant. The notion that this is "purely a business decision and no one has rights over anyone else" is true but irrelevant in light of ethics. I could go on and on about high integrity recruitment but my opinion is very simple and absolute. If you want to do this business ethically, don't fall for the excuses that sponsor shoppers advance. People end up feeling cheated if someone they brought to the table ends up front line to another distributor. Frankly, they should. I have always refused to waiver on that point.

The reason structural integrity works is that everyone has many potential upline partners. In my own case, a guy who wasn't even signed up in our company introduced me to MLM. Once I'd made the decision to participate, I called and asked him to make up his mind quickly so I could sign up on his front line. He signed up but he couldn't coach me properly. Next, I called his upline in another city and he was equally new to our company. When I called that guy's upline, he tried to recruit me into another deal. Instead I called the next person up another level. The fourth call was to a lady who was competent, but we had an immediate personality clash. Her leadership style was authoritarian and I couldn't stomach authority figures.

Finally, I reached Richard Kall, who was positioned six levels above me in the compensation plan. I respected him immediately and he became my life-long coach in MLM. To this day we still talk on the phone regularly because he's a dear friend. We haven't been in business together for the last decade, but nothing could interrupt our close friendship and mutual respect.

Partner Selection

There are several elements that are critical during the business partnership selection phase of networking. First, you want to find a person with whom you share similarities. That person can be different in every respect, but you should feel comfortable with his or her personality style. When I met Richard, the fact that he was a Jewish man from Long Island and I was a Christian minister from Texas became irrelevant because we shared complimentary personality traits.

"MLM has a way of gradually weeding out the non-workers."

I liked him instinctively and respected his ethics immediately. He didn't care that I was six levels beneath him in the comp plan and he was always available whenever I needed help. Before the first two years were finished, four of the six people between us in the compensation plan had quit and eventually all six quit. MLM has a way of gradually weeding out the non-workers. So, while you may begin far below your partner, you'll likely end up closer to him or her during the process of company growth.

Your partner should already be making the kind of money you wish to earn, which is what will allow you to discuss big money with prospects. **Remember, every great network marketer is a lousy network marketer first.** No one starts out earning $50,000 a month. That's why partnerships with upline mentors are so very critical. We have to be able to introduce prospects to folks who are doing what we claim they can do. If distributors immediately above you have no examples of anyone earning good money, how can you possibly introduce prospects to a role model? It is this step in business building that is most valuable. Every new distributor must have an upline partner who can demonstrate the earning potential of the company. Otherwise prospects will assume that the big money is merely a dream.

During the partner selection process you need to focus on finding a person in your upline, somewhere above you in the comp plan, who can demonstrate three things:

- a willingness to talk to your key prospects
- a significant monthly income
- a compatible personality

If no one in your upline meets all three of those criteria, you better look for a different company. That concept may not be real popular with some folks, but I'm not writing this book to win a popularity contest. To follow my system correctly you must have a successful upline partner whom you can trust and respect. If you can't find a winner anywhere above you, the system will not work. That's because a key element of success is third party validation by someone who can honestly demonstrate earnings potential in your company.

Having several successful people in your upline who are unwilling to return calls or talk to your prospects is just as unproductive as having no one in your upline who is successful. In both cases, you are faced with a critical missing link. Besides, if you have no one above you who is successful, what does that tell you about your potential success? Real MLM legends are ALWAYS accessible to their downline partners. This business is about helping others, not building or edifying egos!

Working With Your New Partner

When you contact the individuals above you and find one who is successful and likable, ask her if she will allow you to give her phone number to great prospects. Three-way calling is ideal, but not always practical. (A three way is a telephone call during which you, your prospect and your upline are linked simultaneously.) Ideally, the first few calls you conduct should be three ways so that you can hear your upline in action.

Once you've observed a few, it's then time to simply turn your best prospects over to your upline. You should continue focusing on your first priority, which is prospecting new people. Next I'll cover the step-by-step process for prospecting, but for now I want to make two points:

First, you should be able to trust your upline to never steal a great prospect. The only way to determine his integrity is to send him several great people, then follow up on them. That seems obvious, but MLM companies are crammed with a certain number of people who will steal great leads and many corporate leaders will support them in that effort. It's better to find out early in your career if you can trust your leaders, both field and corporate. If you can't, quit immediately.

Second, don't ever send a prospect who is uninformed about your company to your upline partner. It's not fair to leaders to expect them to spend hours explaining the basics to uninformed prospects. By the time you initiate an upline call, the prospect should have reviewed some of the sales tools and have a basic understanding of the products and compensation plan. Do not waste your partner's time with non-prospects who have no clues about your opportunity.

No one is more important to your success than your upline partner. Without one, you may eventually succeed, but unless you are a remarkable entrepreneur with above average communications skills, your chances are slim. Although everything was in place in my first company, I'll always believe I would have never earned $15 million dollars without partnering with Richard Kall.

Before moving to the next chapter, make certain you have the right upline partner prepared to work with you.

SUMMARY

Having a partner is a critical component in your success during your best year in network marketing. Here are some things you should be aware of:

- Although you recognize the importance of an effective partner, always uphold ethics and your integrity by staying under the person with whom you first signed up – that person who introduced you to the opportunity.

- Always look for a partner who is in your upline and has achieved the success to which you aspire and can teach you things about the business.

- Your chosen partner should have sufficient income to demonstrate the financial potential to prospects.

- Your chosen partner should be willing to talk to your best prospects.

- Your chosen partner should have a likeable personality in order to talk to prospects effectively.

- Ethical partners will never steal any prospects.

- Your partner should be genuinely interested in your success. After all, your partner has a vested interest in you since you are in his downline.

CHAPTER EIGHT

Mindset

"If you aren't passionate before you start, you won't magically 'arrive' after you start."

YOUR BEST YEAR IN NETWORK MARKETING WILL NOT BE THE YEAR in which you earn the most money. Although wealth and popularity tend to be the adult report cards in our world, they have nothing to do with self worth. Worth is a state of mind that has little to do with worldly possessions. I also discovered that "time freedom" in and of itself does not yield a sense of self worth. In fact, the real shocker to me was that time freedom was/is the greatest delusion.

Most of us join MLM because of the lure of passive residual income. The notion that we might leverage ourselves through thousands of other people is appealing. Yet, with respect to self worth, the pot at the end of the rainbow is non-existent. Self worth comes from the doing of something, preferably something that builds and ultimately helps others. Having a bunch of stuff and just passing the time away does not give us that sense of self worth. If anything, we quickly begin to feel very worthless. Let's discuss the basic requirement to succeed in network marketing and life for that matter: *mindset*.

Dr. William Glasser

Before graduation every high school student should be required to read *Reality Therapy* by William Glasser. Dr. Glasser advances the controversial theory that there is no such thing as mental illness. His thesis is that we all have two fundamental needs (obviously, beyond the basic needs: food, water, shelter, etc.): the need to give and receive love and the need to feel worthwhile to others and ourselves. If either of these needs are unmet, we become emotionally and/or mentally troubled or at least unstable, and we're certainly not going to be very happy or content.

Glasser was far ahead of his peers and most of them rejected him because he knew the sad truth about many forms of counseling: namely, long-term therapy was/is designed with the therapist's long-term income in mind. I hate to sound cynical, but I am just stating a fact.

So what if you were potty trained wrongly? So what if your mom didn't hug you enough? So what if your parents were divorced? Does that mean you have to spend the rest of your life in mediocrity, useless to yourself and to others? Of course not. But, I suppose, if you spend $200 an hour to have some psychologist provide you with the notion that past problems resulted in present mindsets, guess what? You'll buy into it. Obviously, many people so want to find a way to legitimize their excuses for mediocrity, they'll gladly pay for them.

The New Mindset

It's time to create a new mental state and prepare for your best year. You need to understand that your past and future are irrelevant. You cannot fail because your past was horrible and you will not succeed based on a future of passive, residual income. The joy of MLM will result from the hardest, most productive time of your life – the time you build for yourself and for others.

I often receive correspondence and telephone calls from people with whom I worked for over a decade in my first MLM venture. Some can't believe that I would be working so hard again after achieving dramatic wealth and time freedom years earlier. They wonder why I can't just kick back and enjoy my last few decades of life in peace and quiet. The answer is simple. We're all about to spend eternity in peace and quiet. I'll rest when I'm dead. Until then, give me a dream and the ability to be productive and my life works. This gives me the sense of self worth I require.

As I explained earlier in this book, I woke up in a gilded cage at age 45 with all the money and free time I needed for the rest of my life. But I began a boring trip into worthless days, lonely nights and meaningless endeavors. Gstaad Switzerland is a fairyland and I lived in the nicest Swiss chalet in that village. I had friends from all over the world who had big money and interesting lives. Every day in the summer I could paraglide to my heart's content and in the winter I was a block from the ski lift. The most important decision I had to make each day was in which gourmet restaurant I intended to dine that night. It actually became a living, boring hell.

"I was willing to put all my wealth at risk and start over building a new dream."

My life was devoid of love and I was doing nothing productive. While some close to me were happy as pigs in slop, I was living in a world of pretense and underachievement. All I could think about was getting back into some kind of ground floor opportunity. I was willing to put all my wealth at risk and start over building a new dream. My partner wanted to protect the assets and be safe. Ultimately the partnership ended in divorce.

I went back to work and formed new partnerships with others who shared my belief in prosperity with purpose. God is just.

Starting Anew

For the first time in a decade my life began to work because I was building a dream for myself and others, not just writing books about the past. Suffice to say it is never very smart to do for others what they should be doing for themselves. You can create an unbelievable nightmare for yourself if you give away money and credit to those who haven't earned it. I've made that mistake many times.

Seldom does a week go by that I fail to meet at least one man or woman who refuses to participate in MLM because they worked for years to build a lifetime income only to have it stolen by a partner they thought they could trust. Many are so bitter that they refuse to see the value in starting over. Yet I know from experience that without a doubt it's the process of building something more than the destination itself that results in joy.

Adopting The Right Mindset

How then does one create the proper mindset for her best year in network marketing and her life? First, commit to and get excited about the dream of building something big. I mean, why commit to something small? Think small?! No. Think big! I saw something big from the beginning. And, naturally, to achieve something big, you must think big. Yes, I was broke when I started out, but I wanted to get into something that had unlimited potential. I figured that if I was going to get involved in something, it may as well be something I could make big. And MLM is definitely something you can make big. But you must think big. Otherwise you put yourself at a psychological disadvantage from the start. That's the purpose behind setting a goal bigger than yourself. And keep in mind, setting a goal of just making big money is not enough. You must also build something for others.

The other thing you need to do so you can adopt the appropriate mindset to approach many, many people, and build that dynasty, is to review your company and products. Be honest with yourself and answer the following questions:

- Will thousands of people experience a benefit (financial or otherwise) once they become involved in your organization?

- Do you truly believe that the distribution of your products to consumers can change the world for the better (e.g., improve the health, the self image, or some other benefit to others)?

- Can you see the possibility of average people succeeding financially by becoming distributors in your downline?

- Are you involved early enough to be a pioneer in your deal or have you figured out a way to renew the potential of an old business?

- Do you respect your corporate and field leaders to the extent that you know they will always do what's right?

- Does your company offer a level playing field in which no "big hitters" will be granted special deals?

- Are you truly excited when you awaken each morning because of the challenges that lay before you?

- Are you willing to bet your future on your company to the extent that you feel comfortable introducing your best friends and family to the products and opportunity?

If your answer to any of those questions is "no," go back and carefully scrutinize your company and products. If you aren't passionate before you start, you won't magically "arrive" after you start. Worse, you probably won't ever achieve the wealth you want if you aren't passionate about the building process. I'm sorry, but I'm just stating a fact.

I suggest that you begin right now reviewing your opportunity once more. When you know the leaders and understand the pay plan, once you've used the products or services and believe in their value, and you are truly passionate about your future, it's time to begin.

Those folks who cannot get excited about any one of those things will not succeed dramatically in an industry that demands passion and enthusiasm in order to succeed. If you cannot find a company about which you are tremendously excited, this business is probably not for you. Because, even if you succeed through sheer determination and will, you won't enjoy the end result if you failed to enjoy the process.

SUMMARY

If you are passionate about your product and company, you are just about ready to launch your best year. In the next chapter, we'll discuss the methods for maintaining the passionate mindset and then it's time to get rolling. Right now, review the following points about the proper mindset to make your dream a reality:

- Forget about the past, and don't worry too much about the future. You build your future now. The fact is, your past may effect you, but it does not have to prevent you from succeeding. Dr. William Glasser is right about this, unlike most of his colleagues. I had a past with nothing but failures until I decided to make the changes necessary to succeed.

- Be prepared to work hard. You have probably heard the adage: Nothing worth having comes easily. Well, it's true. If this were easy, everyone who did it, would become a millionaire.

- You must proceed as a network marketing professional with a passion for your product and company. If you do not, you will not have the success you dream about.

- Study your product and company very carefully. Know everything about both: the history, the background and reputation of the founders of the company, the way the company is organized, the compensation plan, how long the company has been around, the overall attitude of consumers about the product, and so on.

- Be honest with yourself. If you are not sufficiently enthusiastic, or if you are not sufficiently disciplined to follow through, perhaps this business is not for you.

- Get passionate about the building process, not simply the end result. Enjoy the journey.

CHAPTER NINE

Maintaining Your Mindset

"Success in MLM results much more often from attitude than ability."

IT USED TO MAKE ME CRAZY WHEN THEOLOGIANS WOULD PROCLAIM: "The end is near!" I don't believe anyone knows when that time is coming and my analysis of both the Old and New Testament reveals nothing concrete about the end of time. My statement became: "Don't tell me the end is near, just tell me when it's here!" Good news is no news according to television journalists, radio broadcasters, newspaper editors, webmasters, etc. Horrible acts sell. But bad news does not motivate me. In fact, bad news has the opposite effect: it makes me a less effective networker.

To be an effective networker you must be enthusiastic, sincere and believable. You must convey the sense that you enjoy this business, that the products and the opportunity you wish to impart to prospects are the best things for them to pursue. You have heard that enthusiasm is contagious, right? Well, it is. And that's what you want to do: affect people around you with the enthusiasm you have about your product and company.

Rejection & Attrition

One of the greatest challenges a networker has is dealing with rejection and attrition. Most people have difficulty with rejection. After all, it is perfectly normal to want to be accepted. We all want people to respond favorably to what we have to offer, but network marketing can be very discouraging because of the rejection. It's depressing when friends show no interest, or don't even bother to meet with you to hear your presentation. Or you sign up someone who showed tremendous potential, but they lose interest, drop your company to sign up with someone else, or just quit MLM.

"Don't dwell on the rejection or attrition; just keep moving."

The fact is, most people you contact will not sign up. As I said in an earlier chapter, this is a business of numbers. You need to approach many, many people before you sign someone-at least 30 people before you get one. And after you sign people, the attrition rate is still about 75%. These facts can induce negative, counter-productive thoughts, no question about it. Believe me, if anyone knows the effect of rejection and attrition on your mindset, I do. Sometimes it's not easy to get around it. But there are things you can do to maintain your mindset and your productivity.

Don't Dwell On Depression

It may sound overly simple, but when you are depressed or discouraged, and when you are on the verge of giving up, simply move on. Don't dwell on the rejection or attrition, just keep moving. And by all means, don't take it personally. When you get depressed, just tell yourself to stop being depressed and reframe your negative thought into a positive. Be aware of what you're thinking and how you're talking to yourself, and immediately correct your attitude.

Think of it this way, if someone is not interested, or loses interest, at least you have not wasted too much time on them. Go find someone who will be enthusiastic and hang in there. And the fact is, you will eventually find such a person. They're out there. I know, I found them – that's why I've made the money that I have. But you must persevere. And you must maintain a positive outlook based on the fact that even though you have had a series of rejections, or No's, you're just that much closer to a Yes. This may seem like an oversimplification, but it is a fact.

Your Partner/Mentor

To help you maintain a positive mindset so you will persevere for the long-term, calling your upline partner becomes very important. I guarantee you that your partner knows the feelings you have. Talk to them about it. Let them help you put things back into perspective. Remember, as your upline leader, they are very much concerned about your future. They want you to succeed. They don't want you to quit. So, that's why I always say, when down, go upline.

It's by design that I personally make my phone number available to everyone in my downline, and to just about everyone else who wants to talk about our fabulous industry. I want my downline to come to me when they are feeling depressed. I know how debilitating depression and discouragement can be. And I know I can help. The right partner in your company will help you, too.

Don't Poison Your DownLine

As you build your MLM dynasty, make sure that you never let anyone in your downline get the impression that you are discouraged or depressed with the business. It is always important to maintain a positive mindset at all times with those in your organization. If they think you're down, that sort of thing can have serious repercussions and could quite possibly unravel much of what you worked so hard to build.

Special Problems For The Professionals

How does a traditional professional person like a doctor, lawyer, dentist, or the like adopt the right mindset to engage in network marketing? After all, they enter the business with a background of status, a title, and an office. Many of these professionals embrace the opportunity that MLM offers as a way to escape long hours, stress, and questionable pay. But they are accustomed to the status and title, and it can be quite discouraging and depressing when they are shunned by their colleagues, friends or strangers as a result of their involvement in MLM. Moreover, they have to deal with the reality of starting from scratch to build their MLM business. They must be very clear in their own mind about how the business can take them out of their current circumstances and provide the kind of lifestyle they desire so much.

I always urge these professionals to use their position in society to their advantage. Each profession puts people in contact with many prospects. This is definitely an advantage. Also the fact that they are professionals immediately gives them credibility. People are more apt to listen to them about their product and company. It is much smarter for these types of people to be forthright about their new business and not try to pretend that they are just doing this because of their spouse. They should be just as passionate about the product and the opportunity as anyone else.

No News For A Year

Apart from rejection and attrition, the serious networker needs to make a conscious choice right up front – no news for a year. I realize that sounds unacceptable to some people because CNN, the newspaper, and *Time* are routine ways of life. They are invaluable sources of information once you're earning big money because they will give you opportunities to help people in need. But until you are making big money, news is of zero positive value. Hunger, murder, terrorism, starvation, AIDS and earthquakes halfway around the world will keep you subtly depressed about the human condition. So will surfing the web.

The key to maintaining the right mindset in order to build your MLM business is to remain as upbeat as possible, as consistently as possible. You may think that news doesn't affect your performance, but it does in ways you may never be able to measure. You don't believe me? Consider the following example of how the news can effect your mindset. And if you think about it, you'll understand what I mean.

Isolated Bad News

I watched a television documentary recently on the new generation and their involvement in eye, ear and nose piercing. The entire hour explored the world of Raves and numerous young people with horribly deformed skin. These kids were interviewed about their underworld dances and propensity for drugs and self-mutilation. During the course of the documentary in the background was a heavy ongoing beat of the electronic music that presumably influences these kids. The words were angry and the melodies haunting. The inference was that everyone between 12 and 20 was a member of some lost society. They interviewed several guys who spoke about the excitement of fishhooks in their cheeks and how wonderful self-mutilation feels as the pain releases endorphins in the brain. The thesis of the one hour special was that we have no idea how lost and confused many young people are today.

> *"If my entire focus is negative, I'll probably recruit fewer front line distributors and sell fewer products."*

I was disturbed because I must admit that I had not paid attention to that age group. It troubled me to think that an entire new generation was being led down a path of questionable distinction. Like so many other things we see in the media, I wasn't overwhelmed, but I did have a low-grade concern that followed me around for quite some time. Kids will be kids and God knows that as an adolescent in the 60's I did it all. But a little pot and war protesting seemed tame compared to the hopelessness, functional illiteracy, and self-mutilation portrayed in that news program. How would our world survive the migration into adulthood of millions of kids who stick balls in their tongues and fishhooks in their cheeks? In what kind of sadomasochistic direction were our adolescents heading and why had I been so utterly oblivious to this widespread trend? These were the questions that haunted me for days.

Then it dawned on me. I was once again a victim of the very process I've been denouncing – isolated bad news. The truth is I know a great number of young people both in the USA and in Canada. Most don't have black tattoos on their faces or cow rings in their noses. And among the tiny crowd who do, how many of them will walk around in that condition at age thirty?

I was a product of the 76 million baby boomers who threw rocks at bigots and smoked dope to Grand Funk. Many of my friends who are today clergymen, teachers and doctors were protesting Vietnam and running through the streets naked in the 60's and 70's. We called it streaking. Two of the biggest nut cases in our circle of friends now run a treatment center for alcoholics in the Midwest, and one girl who spent a year in a mental institution for an LSD overdose is today a respected veterinarian.

Society is not going to be taken over any time soon by a bunch of teenagers who wear fish hooks in their nipples nor is a near-earth asteroid probably going to wipe out humanity this week. But if my entire focus is negative, I'll probably recruit fewer front line distributors and sell fewer products. Because success in MLM results much more often from attitude than ability, we have to remain consciously focused on those things that we can control.

Eliminating The Bad

The last part of this book provides 25 weeks of positive concepts and affirmations intended to inspire, educate and motivate you during the first six months of your best year in MLM. However, before introducing you to positive concepts it's important to understand the need to eliminate those things which could easily distract you from achieving your goal. As I just said, the worst culprit is news. Nothing will destroy your best year in network marketing more rapidly than a daily dose of rape, terror, murder, earthquakes, global warming and starvation. Corporate sponsors understand the human interest in voyeurism and bad news sensationalism. So that's why they promote negativity while they advertise cars and bubbly brown sugar water.

"Maintaining your mindset – a positive mindset – is absolutely critical."

Now I realize that it might seem that I'm advocating social irresponsibility by encouraging networkers to turn off the news for one year. Quite the contrary. What I am suggesting is that you need one year of extreme focus without the added negative effect of horrible news stories. The fact is, any real significant news, bad or otherwise, will reach you anyway. Your neighbor, a relative or a friend will probably tell you. But the point here is that you really should try to avoid anything negative. Besides, once you're earning a million a year you will actually have the money to make a difference about things that bother you. But to get to that big money, you do not want to pay attention to anything that could distract you and make you depressed.

So turn off all news and spend the next year focusing on your business because your attitude will shine through whether it's positive or negative. When, after a year of news blackout, you decide to once again learn about misery, at least you'll be able to write a check for causes that are important to you instead of just feeling like you can't make a difference.

Maintaining your mindset – a positive mindset – is absolutely critical, but you must be committed to avoiding the unnecessary negatives. You may actually find after a year that you don't need CNN again, anyway.

Reasons To Be Optimistic About MLM

Here are many good reasons why network marketing is such a great industry to be in:

- MLM is virtually risk free- – it requires little if any startup capital. Most businesses require startup money before they even open for business.

- MLM is a business you can operate from your home. This is especially nice for people with children who want to raise them rather than have daycare people do so. It's also great for people who want to work for themselves on their own terms. This business is also good for people who hate to commute to boring jobs.

- There is literally no limit to the amount of money you can make in MLM – doctors, lawyers, etc., can only bill based on the work they perform. Leverage is why in networking you can definitely make more than anyone in any given profession.

- You don't have to be beautiful, nor do you need to have a college education. This is literally an equal opportunity business for anyone willing to apply themselves.

- MLM makes it possible for you to have a great deal of time freedom. With the company taking care of product development, shipping, billing, etc., you don't have to worry about all that. You just keep pursuing prospects and cashing your checks.

- MLM should be fun. There is no need to be stressed. If you are, you're doing something wrong. You're just sharing a terrific product and opportunity with people. It's that simple. And they are either interested or they are not. If they are, great. And if they are not, just move on. No need to live a stressed out life like most people with jobs.

- If you follow my guidelines in this book, it is possible that you can make hundreds of thousands of dollars in one year. Heck, you can make a million a year. But you must follow the general guidance I provide. It's an approach that works – I know, I'm living proof that it does.

- Success itself brings with it recognition and admiration. The MLM industry actually gives you awards and formal adulation. Let's face it, everyone wants the attention, and this just comes with the territory.

- As a successful networker, you will undoubtedly want to share your success globally. So you'll probably travel the world, spreading the good news wherever you go; another one of those wonderful perks of MLM.

SUMMARY

You can maintain your mindset no matter what. At times that may seem impossible, but it is possible. Those who do are the ones that succeed and earn the big money in MLM. Here are points for your review about your mindset:

- You must adopt a positive, enthusiastic, upbeat attitude at all times when engaged in this business. People must believe you enjoy building your business.

- Rejection and attrition are a big part of building your business. It's just like any sales effort, you are going to get many No's. But eventually you will get a Yes. And you will have people who will quit, but you will also have people who are committed, resilient and enthusiastic.

- Don't let yourself get depressed. Simply move on. You can sit and feel depressed, or you can move forward toward eventual success.

- Your partner/mentor can help you maintain a positive mindset.

- Don't say anything that could discourage your downline.

- Professionals should take advantage of their position in society to succeed in MLM.

- To avoid any chance of falling victim to a negative mindset, avoid watching, listening to, or reading the news for one year.

- Focus your thoughts on those things over which you have control. Block negative thoughts out of your mind. They'll simply drain you of precious energy.

- Take stock of all the positive things that come with MLM.

CHAPTER TEN

Your Worst Year in Network Marketing

"Statistically, over one third to half of all networkers will wind up going through divorce."

IT'S ASTOUNDING TO ME THAT NO ONE IN OUR INDUSTRY has taken the time to address an important issue that arises in so many successful organizations – marriage and divorce. I talk to men and women often who tell me the same horror stories about broken relationships and lost fortunes. People lose millions of dollars to partners who yanked their assets during a divorce, often assets that the yanker didn't earn. The purpose of this chapter is to point out a few facts which may assist you in avoiding that plight or in helping others. Some will seem obvious; others are never contemplated until it's too late. Over the last two decades I believe I've heard them all.

Statistically, over one third to half of all networkers will wind up going through divorce. That ratio may be higher among those who are big money earners. But MLM is different from other industries because passive residual income is not like a salary from an office job or profession. It is money which continues to flow to a couple based on continuous efforts by others, even after a couple splits. That's complicated enough to deal with.

Then you have the problem that in every MLM organization you can bet that several downline people have bonded to a particular partner of a married team. The connection has nothing to do with competence; it has to do with relationships. A judge in a divorce court may listen to a parade of people – all with different views. Some people swear that the one spouse did most of the support work, while others swear that the other spouse built the entire downline. In the end, everything becomes muddled in the divorce testimony. Heck, you may even have someone with ulterior motives...like walking off with your ex and your money!

You can see how divorce can quickly complicate things, especially when two people have worked closely together, possibly for years to build a substantial downline. Who worked the most? Or should they just share it equally – 50/50? It depends on the situation and the people involved. In some cases, both parties can agree that they more or less worked equally hard at establishing their business. So arrangements to divide the proceeds as they come in, can be made. But what if that is not the case? What if one person did more to establish the business than the other, and the one who did all the work is not inclined to give half of the future income away?

Trophy Income

I personally know men and women who built dynasties in community property states only to go through a brief marriage during which the trophy was not their spouse but rather their spouse's income. Let's examine this closely. Here's the scenario that arises frequently. Jeff is a divorcee who blunders into a tremendous ground-floor opportunity and spends several years focused on building a huge downline. Because he's alone and the kids are grown, he has time to devote his entire life to MLM. In three years, he's earning $100,000 a month.

Jeff notices that for some reason, beautiful women, the kind who never before found him attractive, are suddenly making long eye contact with him at meetings. Some are very, very attentive. Jeff may begin to consider the possibility that the flirtation is directly linked to his prosperity or he may not. It really doesn't matter now that he can have and enjoy a trophy wife. By the way, this happens just as often to great women networkers who become excited about handsome young men. We all love the attention of beautiful people. That's human nature.

So, whether Jeff acknowledges that he's found a trophy wife and admits to himself that her motivation might be money, or he deludes himself into believing that he's gotten more attractive and sexy over the last ten years, he gets married to his dream woman. What he may learn is that the only trophy in his life is the passive residual income which he created prior to meeting his new partner. Chances are she is already involved in his company and may have even built a small downline which further endears him to her by demonstrating a common interest. The reason they met in the first place is because he is so focused on company activities that he only meets other distributors from his business. His social life revolves around his company.

After their marriage, Jeff immediately begins to integrate his partner into a support role. His new wife starts calling his distributors and building relationships with others. Remember that at the time Jeff and his beautiful soul mate met, the organization was already in place. Many of his front line leaders may even resent the new partner, so Jeff continues to support his front line friends, all the while trying to convince them to accept his new spouse.

A few years down the road, Jeff realizes that the marriage isn't going to work. At that point, he learns the difference between MLM and traditional business: his wife deserves half of everything in the business. Usually it's her attorney who teaches him that reality. He has unwittingly placed her in a position of leadership and there may be dozens of men and women willing to claim that his new spouse was responsible for their success.

The judge doesn't understand that none of the wife's allies were successful networkers prior to the marriage, nor does he understand that the whole downline was built around leaders who were involved long before the wedding. If a skilled attorney can march a mere twenty people out of a twenty thousand person downline through depositions to testify that the new spouse nurtured them – poof! Bye bye, downline. Judges are not likely to understand that a downline in a legitimate company is a self-perpetuating income stream. What exacerbates the problem is that many leaders include their new spouse's name and photos on audio tapes, books and sales aids. The appearance is that the huge income, created long before the wedding, was a joint effort. In reality, this is often not the case.

"Thousands of people have lost some or most of their passive residual income through divorce."

Misplaced Recognition

This scenario is frankly harder on successful women in MLM than on successful men. Sometimes it's not a divorce so much as the false or misplaced recognition that drives leaders crazy. I watched a woman build one of the largest organizations in our company back in the 80's. She slaved long hours and even had to do battle with her skeptical husband. In addition to raising her children, supporting her husband, and doing volunteer work at a local shelter, she created a $20,000 a month income in our company.

A week before our annual convention, her husband kindly decided to join the business. Those of us who knew the truth about what Jane had accomplished by herself were flabbergasted as we watched her husband walk across the stage and jointly accept the award she had won despite him. To our amazement, his acceptance comments sounded like a victory speech by some conquering hero to an adoring public. From that point forward, many distributors believed that the guy did most of the work. They are still married

Your Best Year in Network Marketing

after all these years which, financially speaking, is a good thing for her. If they had gone through a divorce court and he had simply played the video of his awards speech at the convention, the cheering crowd on tape would have misled the judge.

An MLM Divorce

Thousands of people have lost some or most of their passive residual income through divorce. Many become embittered by the experience and never do network marketing again. I know several. So what's a person to do in order to avoid the potential hazards of an MLM divorce?

Unfortunately, there's not a whole lot that can be done prior to the divorce if the MLM downline was launched during marriage. And quite frankly nothing should be done to cheat a contributing spouse out of his or her share. The guy who leaves his wife of ten years because he finds a new MLM deal and wants to avoid sharing the wealth is the kind of person she is blessed to lose. Twenty thousand a month will not cure greed. But many people will go through divorce and re-marry and others will decide to get married after a large organization has been built. It's those folks to whom I wish to address a few words of caution.

In the event of divorce in a community property state, a person is presumably allowed to keep anything they accumulated prior to the new marriage. However, as we have seen, the issues become too muddled once a spouse can pretend that he or she has contributed to or supported the downline. Although it may be a lie, it looks reasonable to the court. Because, keep in mind, most courts usually don't understand the dynamics of MLM.

Pre-Nuptials

Enter the much maligned pre-nuptial. Most people don't want to complicate the chemistry of "new love" by talking about practicality or law. Somehow, it tends to imply an absence of trust and romance. It also implies that the person who brings it up expects divorce to occur. That's the position usually taken by a trophy spouse. Nonsense! MLM is an unusual industry in which those who have nothing to do with success can appear to deserve half of something they didn't create. Because it's a home business and both partners were home, the judge in a divorce court needs to have the truth spelled out in advance of a divorce situation.

In order to prepare for a possible divorce, an event which affects a large percentage of couples, a legal document should be created which defines the existing organization and each leader's name on each person's front line prior to marriage. In the event of divorce, each person should remain in possession of all the income that results from the efforts of those individuals who were recruited prior to the wedding. Those leaders who join a frontline after the wedding will create additional income which should be equally split in the event of divorce. But each partner should be willing, ethically, to relinquish that money which results from the efforts of those who were recruited by their partner prior to the wedding. I'm no attorney, and that's not legal advice, but it is the recommendation of an MLM attorney I highly respect.

A Word Of Caution

If, God forbid, you happen to be introduced to an MLM company after you and your spouse have already decided to get divorced, do not sign up and begin building until the divorce is final. Do Not! Or, you'll get to divide your income for life no matter how huge it becomes and how little your partner contributes.

Words of Advice

I want to conclude this chapter with a couple of other suggestions that you may have never considered. When you create any materials for your organization, whether they are books, audio tapes, brochures, web sites or any other tools, as I stated earlier, don't automatically add the name of your spouse to the covers unless your spouse contributed equally to the work. By unwittingly giving credit to anyone for something they never did, you'll set yourself up for a potential nightmare. You'll also create confusion in the minds of your downline and a future judge. It's tempting to want to appear the perfect couple who do things together, but real leaders don't demand to be credited with things they never did. Couples seldom contribute equally to any endeavor, but can get half of anything that bares their name even if they contributed zero. Trust me on that one.

I realize that this is a touchy subject. That's why you've probably never seen it in other books or articles. People caught in the chemistry of new romance will seldom disturb the euphoria with mundane things like common sense or rational thinking. But for your own good, just let me bring you down to reality for a moment here.

Every year that you live, you grow older. I realize that some people believe that they're like fine wine and most of us are indeed more full bodied and fragrant the older we get. So I hate to be the one to break this news to you, but the truth is this: if you find yourself the object of attention by younger, beautiful people, the $100,000 a month you're earning could be what's most attractive. I know that's almost impossible to believe – but believe it. Even though you're drop dead gorgeous and a mere 48 years old, that twenty-five year old stud may have something in mind besides your irresistible charm. Trust everyone, but cut the cards.

More Words of Advice

The path of MLM is strewn with the skeletons of successful leaders who threw it all away for short-term relationships. Even if you become President of the United States, you can never prevent a partner from publishing your most personal writings once you're mentally incapable of comprehending the invasion of your privacy. Pray that your ex waits until you are too old to care before violating your privacy. Some are too eager to make another buck quickly and may actually publish tabloid type inaccuracies regardless of how demeaned that might make you feel. That's the worst case scenario.

I would never attempt to improve on the words of a great writer like Shakespeare, but I have found one line in his work which needs revision. He once wrote: "Hell hath no fury like a woman scorned." I beg to differ. His comment was sexist and occurred in another era. Update: "Hell hath no fury like a person scorned who has $25,000 a month in passive residual income with which to express that scorn."

In summary, if you're married to a supportive spouse at the time you enter MLM, don't cheat them out of the best alimony and child support that ever existed. If you're married, but divorce has already been planned for some time, wait until it's final before you sign up. If you are single and highly successful in MLM, suggest a pre-nuptial to any adoring future spouse and see how they react. If that concept disturbs them, that means they are willing and eager to grab half of something they never earned. Use a little common sense. Anyone willing to take half of something they never created will probably never become the loving partner you're seeking. Those who act indignant about a pre-nuptial are planning to take something they don't deserve because a pre-nuptial simply acknowledges, in advance, who has built what! If they are insistent on no pre-nuptial and you are still intent on marrying them, why not remove any economic incentive and give your downline income away to charity and start over and build something together.

Some Final Words of Advice

The truth is this: the only real fulfillment in life is building a dynasty, not retiring and being unproductive. One of the best ways to determine the character of the person with whom you've fallen in love is to tell him or her that you want to start over and build something together from scratch. If they agree, you've got a winner. If they don't, you definitely need a pre-nuptial or someone else. Failure to consider these strategies has caused many decent people to spend their worst year in network marketing. I speak with authority.

SUMMARY

It is a sad fact but true: the better part of half of married couples who are in MLM will end up divorcing. Here are some possible outcomes and what to do about them;

- You may have built a sizable MLM business, prior to marriage, and your spouse may have played only a nominal part in the process, since the marriage. Be aware that if a divorce occurs, your spouse could still end up with half the residual income.

- If two people work together to build the business from scratch, it is only fair that they share the proceeds equally.

- Most judges and courts are not versed in the dynamics of the MLM business. So, it is not always easy to make a convincing case that you were the one who made the greatest contribution in building the business.

- If you are about to divorce and you are about to sign up with an MLM company, wait until the divorce is final.

- If you have a substantial downline and you're single, don't think that suddenly you are overly attractive, beautiful or charming – although maybe you are. You're probably more attractive because of your money.

- If you have a substantial downline, make sure you draw up a pre-nuptial agreement with your new spouse. This may not seem very romantic, but it is one way to determine if your prospective spouse is attracted to you or your money.

- To test the true character of your prospective spouse, just tell them you plan on giving all your money to charity, and you want to work with them to build a new downline from scratch.

- Trust everyone, but cut the cards.

CHAPTER ELEVEN

The Unsupportive Spouse or Partner

"If your partner is against you,
who can be for you?"

THE UN-SUPPORTIVE SPOUSE OR PARTNER IS A PROBLEM that must be nipped in the bud or you can forget succeeding in MLM. Every day it seems I hear from some poor man or woman who complains that their spouse or partner is 100 percent opposed to networking. Nothing is worse than a dream stealer in one's own home. Yet some people take their cell phones into another room in order to ask me questions about MLM so that their own spouse won't hear the conversation. They frequently tell me that their partners are livid about their entrance into our industry and that they have to keep quiet about their venture until they start making money. Few will ever be able to pursue success and "start making money" if they have to deal with a partner/adversary.

Lost Sense of Adventure

So, what can you do in such a scenario? How do we proceed with our dreams and goals when our spouse or significant other refuses to support us? What if we've failed countless times? Does the negative spouse have a good reason for being negative and unsupportive?

Those are all realistic questions which have undoubtedly plagued millions of people. Unfortunately they are symptomatic of what happens when a culture of victimhood emerges to replace a nation of winners. America and Canada became great new worlds because husbands and wives climbed onto ships and risked everything for better lives. In effect these people sacrificed themselves to provide a better future for their children's children and in the process they endured great hardships.

If you think MLM is a risk, imagine selling your spouse on the idea of sailing to a new world with nothing but a bushel of pinto beans and two rocking chairs. Wouldn't that be fun? Well, your relatives did just that or worse. Some of them were forced over here at gun point to pick crops and yet some of their decedents are now signing 50 million dollar deals with tennis shoe companies and serving in Congress.

What happened to our spirit, our sense of adventure? That's a very complex question to a multi-faceted social problem which deserves another entire book. But we can address the unsupportive spouse issue in short order. No one else seems to want to, so I will.

Being Honest With Your Spouse

Honesty is the best policy no matter how painful. Many people forget about the circumstances which led them into monogamy in the first place. If you are one of those people, let's review the facts.

There is a pool of several hundred million people from whom your partner selected you. No one else was as important as you were. Your partner liked the way you looked, the way you smelled, the way you talked, the way you thought, the way you walked – even the way you ate. You could do no wrong. You were once the perfect partner. Your dreams and goals made sense and your spouse decided to bet his or her life on them. So what happened? Did you suddenly become a stinking, blithering idiot who can't do anything right? I doubt it. You probably just lost your edge. You probably learned that it's easier to keep peace by avoiding conflict and big time conflict is what occurs when a person joins an MLM company that subsequently goes under. Join ten that go under and God help you when number eleven emerges and you bring up the bright idea of getting involved with it. Conflict with your spouse is likely to rear its ugly head.

Some people hate conflict so much that they stuff their emotions for a decade, then they hire a hit person to dispose of their spouse. Evidently they prefer facing life in prison or death by lethal injection to the conflict that results from healthy confrontation. Watch *Investigative Reports* on A&E most evenings and you'll hear the stories of countless men and women who are spending their lives behind bars after killing a spouse with whom it seemed easier to commit murder than enter dialogue. Nonsense. Honesty is preferable to violence; so is divorce, for that matter.

Walt Disney's Wife

The key is honesty. You were probably a risk taking entrepreneur the day your partner became your partner. You probably haven't changed much. So why is it so impossible to convince your significant other to support you in some new business venture? How did Walt Disney keep his wife's support? The guy went bankrupt twice trying to build a mouse theme park. Of all the stupid dreams, Disneyland must have seemed, well, the most Mickey Mouse of all! What made Walt continue? More important, what made Walt's wife continue with him?

According to the accounts I've read, Walt Disney was honest and passionate. I suspect there were times when Disney had to resell his wife on Mickey Mouse. He probably had to have a pep talk with her the first time lenders repoed their cars and home. In fact, the second time that the Disneys lost everything, I'll bet Walt had to face a wee bit of negativity. But he didn't quit and his wife didn't quit either. And according to the accounts I've read, she was a very intelligent, headstrong woman. But Walt had a dream and his passion exceeded all family skepticism.

The Failure Factor

The first thing you must do is remind your partner that failure is the best teacher and fully accept your part in failure rather than blaming others. Generally, we don't learn from early success, nor do we value it. Many Lotto winners go bankrupt because they risked nothing for wealth and are soon back to being broke. Each time a man or woman fails, the lessons learned are invaluable steps along the path to success. So, first of all, you may need to remind your partner that you were once the greatest potential partner in the world and that you still can be, provided that you have their support. Next, you need to remind them that failures are learning experiences. You may fail another ten times before succeeding, but so what? Success is worth it. In fact you may both discover, as I did, that the process of striving is far more fun than arriving.

Ask For Support

Sit down with your partner and tell him or her the truth. Ask them confidently and passionately to support you in your new venture. Remind them of your past commitments to each other. Be truthful, open and ask for their support. If you can't reason with them gently, get to a counsellor and examine your relationship. Sometimes it helps to have a trained professional serve as an impartial advisor or listener. An inability to obtain support from your spouse may be symptomatic of a much deeper problem.

Some people actually thrive on conflict. It's rare, but some folks are more concerned with winning than being right. It's a crazy-maker to those of us who prefer peace and it's virtually impossible to find serenity in a relationship in which your spouse thrives on conflict.

Present Your Argument

It's also fair for your partner to ask you a few simple questions about your new venture – things you should know anyway. For example: Who are the owners of the new MLM company and how many times have they succeeded in the past? How much capital does the company have? How much is your sponsor earning? Is the product unique and patented or just another Internet scam? What do you intend to do this time different that didn't work before?

Those are fair questions and deserve honest answers. If they anger you or you can't answer them positively, you might want to look around for a better opportunity. Once you've failed a few times your partner has every right to feel that you aren't just jumping into another money game or doomed upstart. If you can't introduce your spouse to someone in your future upline who is earning big money and comes across extremely honest and supportive, he or she probably has good reason for feeling skeptical. Rejection by a spouse is a very significant cause of failure in an entrepreneurial venture. On the other hand, your spouse may turn out to be your greatest ally if the right questions are asked.

What If You Still Don't Get Support?

Once you've tried everything within reason to earn your partner's support and still failed, even though the venture is solid, it's time to ask yourself the big question. Is my relationship, regardless of its state, worth more than my dream to succeed as an entrepreneur? That's up to you. It's not the kind of question anyone can answer for you but it is the kind of question you should answer for yourself, especially if you find yourself in a miserable position. I have always believed that human relationships are infinitely more important than any other lifetime objective. But when conflict and withholding become the tools a spouse uses to refuse to support their partner, when being right is less important than winning an argument, when ridicule and condemnation replace nurturing and support, it's time to revaluate your relationship.

Don't get nasty, just hand this book to your partner and ask them to read this chapter. The fact that you want to both love your partner and achieve your dreams is a reasonable request. The fact that you may have failed a few times is no excuse for your partner to stomp on your dreams, if you've learned from your mistakes. You may not be as attractive as a movie star and you may not have a fancy degree. You may never have been athletic or a good dancer. You may chew your food goofy and drive your car like a spastic. But your partner made a choice and that person had over 100 million options. We had a saying back in Missouri: "You brought her, now you dance with her!" On the other hand, it's far better to leave a horrible marriage with half your assets than remain and lose your whole mind. Trust me on that one.

SUMMARY

Support from your spouse or partner is another critical component of success in network marketing. Without your spouse's support, you won't get anywhere. When approaching a critical, unsupportive spouse, consider the following:

- Make sure you are well informed about the networking opportunity you're considering.

- Approach your spouse with patience and honesty.

- Acknowledge your past failures, but point out the advantage of failure as a learning experience.

- Allow your spouse to ask you very specific questions concerning the opportunity you want to pursue and remain open to answering them honestly. Take advantage of this as a second chance to make sure this opportunity has a solid foundation and the risk you're taking is well thought out and calculated.

- Ask your spouse for their support in this new endeavor.

- Should they withhold support on a solid business venture, maybe you've got bigger fish to fry.

CHAPTER TWELVE

Brain Change Concepts

DURING A RECENT TRAINING SESSION, immediately following two hours in which I covered the very material discussed in this book, a gentleman raised his hand and asked a predictable question. It comes up every time I train networkers, especially in the college certification class I've taught for ten years at the University of Illinois. He asked: "So, how do we train our people once they sign up as distributors?" My answer is always the same: "That's what you just spent two hours learning. Teach them to follow the process I just taught you."

The purpose of this book is to provide you with training so that you can enjoy your best year in network marketing. How? Well, take these ideas, use them, and teach others to use them. If you don't want to recommend this book, create an outline based on these principles and train from it. I don't care. But what I want you to understand is that what you just read is training. How you choose to teach it is up to you. Some will recommend this book. Many companies will make it available in their kits. Some of you will do a weekly training call, during which new distributors learn your system by telephone. Some may use the internet, while others will train front line people in their own living rooms. It doesn't matter how or where you train. What matters most is that you use the ideas in this book as a starting point and as guidance because they work. That's how you train people. I learned these concepts from numerous legends in our industry and made them my own. Now I'm suggesting you do the same.

Equally important is learning to train your thinking, which I call "brain training." What you and your leaders need more than additional systems is a significant brain map and state of mind. Like most folks, until now, you probably have not had a million dollar a month brain. Paul Orbison did. He got to one point three million dollars a month selling long distance service that was more expensive than half his competitors. Why? He had the right brain.

For the next twenty-five weeks, I'm asking you to focus on my twenty-five brain change concepts. These are the twenty-five ideas you'll need to anchor into your mind in order to achieve no less than $10,000 a month. And even more important, these new brain changes will help you get ready to handle that wealth. Believe me, you'll need more values and intellectual strength in two years once you've hit the big numbers than you do now.

So here's how to use the next part of this book. If you're ready to rock and roll, start with brain change number one and read it every morning and evening for seven days. The best times are soon after you first get up and the last thing you do before you drift off at night. Do your best to think carefully about how your life might change should you apply the weekly thought. No magic here.

Now, I don't care if you believe these ideas or not. Read them and think about them and apply them. Memorize each affirmation and repeat it numerous times for one week. In twenty-five weeks, you should be to the point of earning at least $10,000 a month. But if you're not earning at least $10,000 a month, you have not adopted the ideas in this book. It's that simple. Or, if you have done **everything** suggested in this book, including approaching large numbers of prospects, and you have read, learned and applied the brain changes presented here, and you still are not earning at least $10,000 a month, find a better company, better products, and a better compensation plan. Because, as much as this might anger some people, including your upline, either you are not cut out for MLM or you are in a lousy company with lousy products, if you can't earn ten grand a month, in half a year.

The only exception to this six month/$10,000 per month rule is the person who has no desire to earn big money. Of course, you have just read the wrong book and wasted valuable time if your goals are minimal.

Week One
Passion For MLM

"Passion is more volatile than fossil fuels." Mark Yarnell

People are confused about how anyone can join a 20-year-old company and still make money. I had dozens of calls in 2001 when an industry magazine printed a cover story profiling successful people who recently joined old MLM companies. Many wonder if the value of "ground floor" is a myth like the magazine blatantly asserted.

Unfortunately in their article and leader profiles they failed to emphasize the fact that those who manage to succeed in an older company are in possession of a secret weapon not owned by the masses. It's called passion. Armed with passion about any product or company, an average person can make millions in our industry. Conversely, get in on the ground floor of a future dynasty and unless you are passionate you'll likely quit or fail. Passion is the great equalizer *especially* if you insist on joining an older company.

If you aren't earning at least $10,000 a month in MLM once you've been seriously involved for a year, you're not passionate. If you don't wake up excited every day because you know you are going to get your product into people's hands and dramatically change their lives, you aren't passionate. And if you aren't passionate - get involved in something that makes you leap out of bed each morning, shouting, "Thank You God For This Opportunity!"

When selling MLM magazine subscriptions, the goal is often to profile big, old companies with millions of distributors who will buy reprints of the article. That's called capitalism, and it's why that magazine profiles older companies.

But beyond the self-serving nature of appealing to huge databases, I believe the magazine was right. You can even make money in a 30-year-old deal, armed with one attribute – passion!

Affirmation

"I am passionate about my opportunity and I spring forth today with mighty enthusiasm."

Week Two
Commitment To Your Company

"Don't even begin what you intend to do for less than two years."
Mark Yarnell

One week we got a fax from a lady who requested info about our new MLM company. She didn't have time to call us because her husband was busy doing 3-way calls for the company they were in currently. She wanted to know how many quick-start packs she would need to buy in order to earn $1,000 a week.

My response was swift and decisive:

"MLM is about distribution, not garage qualifying in one deal after another."

It's truly amazing how the MLM mindset has changed over the past decade. People hop from deal to deal then blame their failures on our industry. The key to long-term success is very simple. Find a great company, a great upline, a product you love then go to work full time and make a two-year commitment. Don't look at any other company and don't treat our industry like a part time hobby. This is a profession, not a little Biz! Those of us who make it to the pinnacle aren't more educated or articulate than others; we are more committed and more resilient. MLM is about long-term focus, not short-term opportunism. Leveraged income becomes passive, residual income in those companies that market consumable products or services. No one ever bought his way to lasting income in MLM.

Affirmation

"Today I succeed dramatically by confidently asking dozens of people to purchase my products and/or join my business venture."

Week Three
Attitude

"For a man to achieve all that is demanded of him he must regard himself as greater than he is." Goethe

I agree totally. We live in an era when psychologists actually have a name for a mental affliction describing those who think they are greater than they really are. It's called delusions of grandeur. But the truth is this: a person must have grandiose objectives to ever reach high levels of accomplishment. I have a saying I've always subscribed to and it's one I hope you adopt: "Nothing is too good to be true."

In my opinion, you cannot have dreams and aspirations which are too grand. Nothing is too grand, no amount of money is too much, no amount of personal joy and serenity is too much for those who dare to dream – for those who aspire to what I call Self-Wealth. Figure out exactly what you want and you will succeed! More importantly, you deserve to rise to levels you never dreamed possible.

Affirmation

"I recognize my birthright and move forward this week with a mighty enthusiasm toward dramatic prosperity and personal fulfillment."

Week Four
Big Money For Good Reasons

*"It is well to remember that the entire population of the Universe,
with one trifling exception, is composed of others."*
Andrew Holmes

Nothing is more critical to one's success than helping a bunch of other people get what they're after. In fact, Zig Ziglar built a career around the whole idea that if you just help enough people get what they want, you'll eventually get what you want. I agree.

In the last century, the 80s were called the "Greed Decade." Everybody was running around shouting "me, me, me!" And what was the net result? Many people wound up doing time in federal penitentiaries. Bankers, lawyers, CPAs and many other professionals ruined themselves and their families. Why? Because self-centered, greedy behavior cannot result in long-term success.

If you want to earn more money than you can possibly spend and live a balanced serene life, pay attention to our number one Self-Wealth principle: create a goal bigger than yourself. Plan to give away $50,000 a month to a worthy cause about which you are passionate. This is the week to select a specific passionate cause and commit a huge amount of money. No more lip service.

Remember, other than one exception, the entire universe is composed of others. Figure out what you can do for them and your own life will fall into place.

Affirmation

"I am focused on achieving dramatic wealth and using it to leave my world a better place."

Week Five
Enthusiasm

"Success results much more often from attitude than ability."
Dr. Norman Vincent Peale

For the past year, I've enjoyed the process of observing the emergence of a new MLM company that may be the next billion dollar international dynasty. Many industry legends have chosen to get involved, as have a number of completely inexperienced business builders. The official launch actually occurred in September 2000, but distributors were permitted to actively recruit in early July. It was astonishing to witness the young novices out-recruiting the veterans at a rate of nearly ten to one.

So impressed was I with these statistics that I began calling several of the veterans and the novices to try to understand the phenomenon. As expected, the difference all boils down to attitude. The legends lacked the energy and enthusiasm to truly motivate others to take action while the new people were on fire with contagious enthusiasm.

Doc Peale was right. So was John Wesley when he wrote: "Catch on fire with enthusiasm and people will come from miles to watch you burn." If ability has let you down, try enthusiasm. Few can resist the temptation to partner with an enthusiastic person. This week, focus on adjusting your attitude.

Affirmation

"I am on fire with enthusiasm because I am in an unlimited opportunity and no one can slow my momentum."

Week Six
Fear And Risk

*"I would rather die hang gliding at age 60 than
playing bingo at 90."*
Mark Yarnell

That's the first quote in a book I will eventually publish called *Thoughts From A Simple Country Boy.* From a very early age, I became aware of how people die. After a whole slew of relatives passed away in rest homes with oatmeal dribbling down their chins, I realized that most of them ended up "over the hill" without having ever reached the summit. What really struck me as a young child was that they all died and that my odds of doing the same were one out of one. That's when I concluded that there is no such thing as risk. The only uncertainty about death is "when." The hefty bag of death is always edging closer!

I suggest that you get rid of the petty phobias which bind you to mediocrity. If you have an unwarranted fear of anything, do it. The ancillary benefits of facing phobias and conquering them far outweigh the dangers. Don't just read this brain changer, smile stupidly, then proceed with your life safely. Go whitewater rafting, dare to bungee jump, look up paragliding in the yellow pages and take a flight with a certified tandem pilot. Get out and live before you die. Otherwise you'll march off into eternity with "Under the B-15" ringing in your ears.

Affirmation

"I take calculated risks with confidence and achieve abundant prosperity as a by-product of overcoming all phobias."

Week Seven
Commitment

"Any system works powerfully – if you do." Mark Yarnell

Nearly two decades of networking have taught me that no one has the best strategy. I still hear about why certain systems are better than others and why duplication is so important. Nonsense.

I know dozens of people who are all building substantial downlines and no two are using the same strategy. Some use ads, some use warm lists and some cold call. But, regardless of their differences, the winners are spending ten or twelve hours a day recruiting new distributors. They aren't acting like minimum wage babysitters trying to drag others across the finish line.

Winners don't get stuck in the process of managing people. Nor do they build organizations for others. The reason America has become a nation of victims is that so many people refuse to accept responsibility and so many others are willing to do everything for victims.

If you want to run ads – great! If you want to join a lead generation program – great! If you want to create a web site that builds prospects – great! But I'd like to offer you a little advice. Until you're earning more money than you can spend, work harder than you've ever worked in your life to personally sponsor and train new distributors. Go wide fast!

And above all else, don't ever let yourself become the lingering shadow of a formerly great networker by sitting around treading water, worrying about how to preserve a shrinking check. The fun of MLM is the passion of the build, the excitement of the possibilities that lie ahead.

Any system will work if you passionately approach a dozen or more new prospects each day with the greatest opportunity in free enterprise. And if you don't believe that describes your company, *no* system will work powerfully!

Affirmation

"This week I am emotionally invested and 100 percent committed again to the greatest opportunity in free enterprise: my own."

Week Eight
Tenacity

"We can swallow anything and digest anything you throw at us, turn it into fertilizer and make it a growth experience."
Bernie Siegel, MD

Sounds like a network marketer's motto, doesn't it?

Think about it. If you show tenacity and the ability to adapt to challenges and turn them into learning experiences, you can move forward with passion and enthusiasm.

No matter how many mentors you have, how many tapes you listen to, or books you read about how to build your business, no one except YOU can provide the energy to move forward. The energy you need comes from power, and power comes from inspiration. What's inspiring you to succeed in your business?

When you are sufficiently inspired, you'll face all the challenges head on, change, grow, adapt and develop new abilities. You'll do whatever it takes, I repeat, whatever it takes, to walk that extra mile.

Stay with it, my friends. Develop your passion and look for the growth experience in every challenge.

Affirmation
"I simply convert every challenge into a stepping stone and move forward with passion and joy."

Week Nine
Mentors

"No one ever learned anything while talking."   Mark Yarnell

I'm amazed at the number of calls I get from individuals who claim they want to be coached properly. Before I can provide them with any steps to success, many feel the need to launch into an in-depth description of all their failures and successes. I let them continue for five or ten minutes and then interrupt them by beginning to explain the systems that work. Usually I get less than a minute of dialogue in before they begin interrupting me with arguments about my ideas.

First, they make excuses about why they can't call their warm market. Next, they challenge my shotgun recruiting or the wording in my cold market approach. Then they tell me why the Internet is the best lead generation system available.

On and on they go, ad nauseum. It's easy for me to now understand what allowed me to earn millions in MLM while most people jump from failure to failure. I simply called Richard Kall, asked him to mentor me, then shut up.

Success in our industry often results from common sense. If someone in your upline is earning ten times as much as you, don't waste their time with war stories about yourself. Learn what they are doing and duplicate it. Either shut up, or keep talking and fail. Simple enough.

Affirmation
"I am open and receptive to the coaching of my mentor."

Week Ten
Having Courage

"Risk is inherent in any action. The key to an effective economy is confidence." Alan Greenspan

I once listened to Mr. Greenspan lecture a congressional finance committee about what is needed to sustain growth in an economic downturn. Instead of cutting interest rates or implementing some complicated formula for strategic change, he stated the obvious.

When people are willing to ignore risk and confidently move forward in spite of fears, great things happen. Yet, in our industry, most individuals move cautiously and approach tiny numbers of prospects without passion or confidence.

If Alan Greenspan, the genius of US economics, believes that confidence and the willingness to take risk will allow the entire economy to blossom, he's absolutely right. But imagine how dramatically our economy could prosper if all working people were given the capacity to triple their income every month.

In MLM, that's the rule and not the exception. Outfitted with nothing more than the courage to face call reluctance and a bit of confidence, anyone in MLM can triple their income by tripling their efforts.

If you talk to three times as many prospects, you'll earn three times more money. If you approach three times as many customers, you'll sell three times more products. No one can stop you; in fact, no one can even slow you down.

Try this simple experiment. Be honest with yourself. Take the number of people you approached last month and increase that number three times next month. When you get your next check, you'll understand the power of personal confidence. If it's good enough for the country, it's good enough for you and me.

Affirmation

"This week I triple my efforts and therefore my income."

Week Eleven

Dealing With Criticism

*"Even if a thousand people believe a stupid thing,
it's still a stupid thing."* Mark Yarnell

But what happens when one person believes a stupid thing? Some people react to uninformed criticism immediately, especially in Network Marketing.

Often, in their quest to avoid an unlimited MLM opportunity, prospects will surface ridiculous objections. Or, new distributors who have done very little, if anything, will become overly critical about some obscure elements of a product, company or comp plan. The trap into which even the best leaders often fall is the waste of focus and energy that occurs when a negative person diverts us into an area of worthless minutiae. There are some simple rules which can keep us productive in "stupid" circumstances.

First, prospects haven't earned the right to be critical of your opportunity. Until they've signed up, been trained and gone to work, they don't really have the wisdom to provide constructive criticism. Listen cordially, and then go back to work.

Second, until new distributors have proven their loyalty and achieved a few months of productive retailing and team building, they haven't earned the right to begin criticizing anything. Gently guide them back to work.

Don't be tempted to waste your time by focusing on such people's suggestions. Sell your product, sell your opportunity and don't worry about critics who haven't earned the right to divert your focus.

More often than not, such criticism is unfounded. When prospects or new distributors are attempting to defend, rationalize and justify their motives for inactivity or failure, they will always point the finger at anything or anyone other than themselves. Coach them through it, act as a role model and carry on like any great leader would. Don't argue; merely demonstrate what's possible.

Affirmation

"I prosper dramatically by ignoring those who criticize my opportunity or product."

Week Twelve

Rejection And Excuses

"When people say "no" they don't mean "yes." Mark Yarnell

Network Marketing is a challenging profession that demands a certain kind of person. Above all else, networkers require a tremendous self-image and a pioneering, risk-taking mentality. Most people don't succeed because they don't have the talent. So, when prospects say "no" after you've given them your best shot, move on.

Most people don't ever attempt to rise to their full potential and many are frightened tremendously when faced with an unlimited network marketing opportunity. The last thing you need to do is argue with such a person or set up a three-way with your upline.

The faster prospects that don't have the talent say "no," the better off you are. It's those folks who pretend they are interested and then drag you and your upline through needless conversations that are your worst problem. When people say "no" in the first five minutes, respect their objections and understand that they mean "no."

I have five or six "chronics" who contact me every two or three months with a new excuse. They are just about ready to be wealthy and they know everyone in the world. Once they finish one more project, read one more book, or once I send them just "one more bit of information," they are going to sign up and drive this deal to the moon. Bull.

Some prospects will never have the courage to say "no." And that brings me to my final point: when people say "yes," unless they go to work immediately, they don't always mean, "yes." Actions speak much louder than words.

Affirmation

"I support those who demonstrate a willingness to work and refuse to argue with those who do not."

Week Thirteen

Avoiding Self-Defeat

"The greatest opponent we face in networking is our own inner critic." Mark Yarnell

Be on the lookout for self-sabotage because it's your inner critic at work and you can consciously control it. By self-sabotage, I mean those golden business opportunities you don't follow up on, the phone calls you neglect to return, or the invitations you turn down that could move you closer to success.

My favorite self-sabotage fable is the one about the man who is caught in a flood. As the water rises, a fire fighter comes by in a big truck and offers him a ride. "No," he says. "I have faith in God. He will save me."

Meanwhile, the ground floor of the man's house is flooded, forcing him to climb up to the next level. A police officer offers him a boat. "No, I have faith in God," he tells her.

Soon the man is on his rooftop surrounded by water, at which point a helicopter circles overhead. A rope is dropped and the rescue team implores him to grab on. "No, God will save me," he shouts. A short while later, the house is destroyed by the flood and the man drowns.

The man stands at the pearly gates of Heaven, in shock. He asks, "How could God let me, a true believer, drown?" He hears a voice thundering from above. "First I sent you a truck, then a boat, and then a helicopter. What more did you want, my friend?"

The inner critic tries to keep us stuck in old ways of thinking and believing, and denies opportunities to grow our business. Instead of recognizing them as opportunities, we tend to stay in a safe rut and deny them.

That same critic looks for confirmation and support daily. If someone we prospect declines to participate, our inner critic shouts gleefully, "See, she thinks this is a stupid idea, too." Or it might

---

say, "Your neighbor's right, this dream of yours will never happen." It's this incessant critical voice that often causes us to sabotage our own success.

If you deal with that inner critic effectively, you'll be able to take on others who try to discourage you. Be aware of what you're thinking throughout the day and stop the negative thoughts.

Affirmation

"I silence my inner critic and focus only on those thoughts which inspire me to take positive action."

Week Fourteen

Commitment To Your Opportunity

"MLM vampires lurk behind every bush." Mark Yarnell

Even the most skilled and loyal networkers must be armed for the focus battle. Yesterday I got a fax that announced the "ground floor end of long distance." No more bills of any kind – zero fees. They wrote that I should be ready for my launch kit in an unlimited width opportunity that half of America will join in less than a month. The sender was very skilled and articulate and the fax created a lot of curiosity.

Then I stopped long enough to apply a little common sense. Usually a few simple questions will do: Where's the commissionable volume in a zero-cost long distance company? Which tracking company has the software to place 150 million people in a pay plan virtually overnight? Who are the owners? How much capital do they have? Which MLM lawyers wrote the legal opinion on their compensation plan?

It takes a minimum of five years intense focus in one company to make the truly big money in network marketing. So let me give you some sound advice. Any time a new opportunity comes to you by any means, especially email or fax, hold up a mental bag of garlic as if a financial vampire were attacking you. The reason most MLMers are walking around like zombies from *Night of The Living Dead* is that they jump on every new deal that comes across their path. Throw away anything that is irrelevant to your current business.

Affirmation

"I am closed to all opportunities except the one to which I am committed."

Week Fifteen

Best Recruiting Methods

"Capitalization" rather than "duplication." Mark Yarnell

Last millennium, people believed that the key to success in MLM was duplication. I wrote about it myself in two books that are now obsolete. The real key to success in this new century is figuring out the assets of new distributors and then helping each person build a lucrative business by capitalizing on their strengths.

Some people have a huge card file full of thousands of former clients or customers, while other new distributors have been successful using direct mail marketing systems. Others are most comfortable approaching prospects with audios at public events. Some write great ads and belong to lead generation companies.

The point is that a great leader will ask enough questions of a new distributor to determine that person's unique talents for retailing, recruiting and coaching. I believe everyone should begin by contacting those in their warm market, but beyond that strategy, upline leaders need to help new people figure out a building system best suited to their own talents and personalities.

No single system is duplicable for every personality type. Extroverts and introverts are both capable of succeeding in our industry so long as their uplines assist them in taking advantage of their own unique gifts.

Affirmation

"This week I am focused on helping each front line distributor capitalize on his or her unique assets in order that they might effectively go wide fast."

Week Sixteen

Strategic Prospecting

"Go get 'em!" Mark Yarnell

According to a recent US Census report, the number of self-employed people over the age of 16 has risen from 7 percent to 10.35 percent since 1970. That means that nearly 90 percent of all working people in America are employed – that means "dependent." That is such a huge market for MLMers and yet we still spend countless hours trying to grab our share of the 10 percent of the population who are already independent. Duh!

If you want to truly remove yourself from the competition, stop competing for that same 10 percent of the population. It used to be that a "big hitter" in our industry was a person earning $300,000 a month who had been in one company for at least five years. Today, a big hitter is anyone who is broke with fifty leads.

A guy called me this week who has personally sponsored 25 people in 10 days. When I asked him how he did it, he simply said he's looking for people who've never been in MLM. In fact, if a prospect has ever been involved in any other company, he immediately moves on to someone else. That's how he qualifies prospects.

We have a country in which 90 percent of the people are miserable, dependent employees who don't read home business ads because they are too tired after 12-hour days of working and commuting. Go get 'em!

Affirmation

"This week I focus my efforts on those millions of people who have never been involved in MLM."

Week Seventeen

Passion About Your Company

"Introducing the best MLM in history." Mark Yarnell

In my opinion, there is now only one legitimate MLM Company out there. The comp plan has emerged as the best ever created. The owners are ethical and have enough capital to do this business right. The field leaders are loyal and committed to excellence. The marketing tools are exceptional and the company will obviously be around for decades.

Now that the company is more visible, I'm shocked that some people are in other deals because this opportunity is far superior. Those of us who understand MLM are astounded at the growth potential of this company. In fact, given all the elements necessary for long term success and the fact that this networking dynasty now has them all in place, I can't imagine it not becoming a multi-billion dollar giant.

If there's only one downside, it's that some of its most dynamic leaders don't yet understand just how lucky they are to be involved. Once they put on blinders to every other opportunity out there, this company will surpass most others in yearly sales.

Anyone who recognizes what I've seen, buckles down and goes to work full time, and puts on blinders to every other MLM out there is destined to become filthy, stinking rich. The company? Yours, once you see it!

Affirmation

"I am passionate, committed and enthusiastic about my company and I prosper in direct relation to my passion."

Week Eighteen

Let Experience Teach You

"The wheel has never been reinvented. If you want to really become prosperous, ask a person who's made it to the top to coach you and then be quiet and listen." Mark Yarnell

No one is more valuable to the MLM leader than a mentor who has achieved a significant degree of success. And remember, great people cannot resist the temptation to tell their stories to people who ask for their help. The key is to not only ask a person for help, but then to follow their coaching, even if it seems unconventional. Most paths to success are very unconventional and often seem unworkable; that's precisely why only a handful of people follow them.

Success in MLM is about effort, not shortcuts, but there is one tremendous shortcut to the top. Find a person more experienced than you and follow exactly what they teach you. Oh, and by the way, once you've created Self-Wealth, be unselfish about mentoring others when they seek your coaching.

As a mentor, you will eventually be able to evaluate the assets of each new distributor then coach her accordingly. Great mentors see more in their protegé than the protegé sees in themselves.

Affirmation

"I listen and follow the coaching of my upline mentor and prosper abundantly."

Week Nineteen

Teamwork

"More people die from ridicule than from guns." Anonymous

The great emotional plague of humanity has always been our willingness to attempt to elevate ourselves by denigrating others. Unfortunately our negative assessment of other people is never profitable and usually devastating to others. It serves absolutely no purpose to talk unkindly about others, whether we happen to believe we're right or not. It's especially true in professional networking where each time a company or individual distributor fails, it brings down our entire industry another notch.

May I encourage you to adopt a simple philosophy? If you wouldn't write it down and sign it for the entire world to read, don't say it. Ridicule is a killer. And to those of you who become the recipients of criticism from others who have nothing better to do than attack their brothers and sisters, remember this: the best revenge is a life well lived. Critics are so busy writing and talking negative that they have no time to create anything.

I was privileged to hear the Dalai Lama speak in Los Angeles several years back and he made one comment worth the entire evening. He said, "My friends, if you can't help other people, would you please not hurt them." Great advice for network marketers.

Affirmation

"I lift others up and empower them through speaking kindly to them and about them."

Week Twenty

Recruiting

"The mind is not a vessel to be filled but a fire to be ignited."
Plutarch

If there is one common mistake many networkers make, it's taking a simple concept and making it unnecessarily complex. People don't need their minds filled with facts and figures calculated to inform them about product ingredients, comp plans, new services, corporate leadership credibility, web sites, fax-on-demand info, sales tools and future expansion. The more information we provide to prospects, the more likely they will ignore our opportunities.

Prospective distributors are interested in two things: how to earn the most money possible and how to achieve more time freedom to spend with family and friends.

Our goal should always be to ignite their enthusiasm with the excitement of big money and time freedom. It's not that people are stupid; it's just that they won't get excited about facts on product ingredients and technical comp plans.

Try one month of prospecting during which you simply talk to people about unlimited financial potential and time freedom. Then send them to a conference call, sizzle call or informational web site AFTER you have captured their curiosity. Simple enthusiasm is what ignites the minds of others, especially in the initial encounter.

Affirmation

"Today I succeed dramatically by discussing wealth and time freedom passionately with everyone I meet."

Week Twenty One

Ignoring Egocentric Prospects

"God made the birds and the worms, but He didn't go around dumping worms in nests." Mark Yarnell

One day a prospect told me that he was being flown into three different companies in order to meet with the corporate leaders. He said he would be happy to talk to anyone, but first wanted to know how many front line people would be placed under him and how many leads he would be provided each month.

He explained that he was a "big hitter" with 30,000 people in his last downline in another deal that had just gone under.

I told him I wouldn't give him any leads, any front line people and that he wouldn't be flown into the home office. He was absolutely indignant, so I wished him the best of luck and hung up.

He called back an hour later in total disbelief that I wasn't overwhelmed with his potential. He wanted to know why I didn't want to work with someone of his stature. Since you will eventually bump into this kind of person, I'll print my exact response so you can use it on your own egomaniac prospects.

I said, "Phil, the only thing we know about you for sure is that you don't know how to pick a good company. We also know that you are willing to recruit others into deals that go under. If a company is legitimate, they won't spend their revenue wining and dining non-distributors. Great companies reward their loyal distributors, and not arrogant prospects. We want people who are looking for a home and not a free meal. The fact that you are asking for leads and a plane ticket is proof to me that you won't fit into our culture." At that point he stopped me and interjected, "yeah, but I could make you a fortune! Aren't you being stupid?"

I said, "Maybe, Phil. But I don't want to spend the next 20 years of my life socializing and working with people who need to be dragged over the finish line. I don't have to buy friends or associates.". He hung up on me.

Affirmation

"I earn my way to greatness through massive, daily action and expect the same from all with whom I associate."

Week Twenty Two

Productive Effort

"In the heaven of unfulfilled dreams, the lives we might have led sit silently and face eternity with no hope." Mark Yarnell

It must be terrible to awaken at an older age and come face to face with the fact that no personal dreams have been achieved. Of course, it must be worse for networkers than any others because we have no limits on our dreams. Except, that is, for those who choose money games over legitimate MLM companies, or those who decide to consult instead of building a business. Professional networkers need not worry about "the lives we might have led."

There is one exception to that rule. It's the person who joins a legitimate company with great products and a lucrative compensation plan at the right time and then spends an entire career in activities designed to avoid productivity. Listening to tapes, studying the comp plan, and conducting or leading weekly in-home meetings are all designed to look like effort. They aren't. If our goal is to lead by example, we must spend the majority of our time talking to potential customers and prospects. Time spent planning is wasted. It takes me an hour or two each January to write down goals and the rest of the year to achieve them.

Those in salaried jobs have plenty of excuses for why they die with unfulfilled dreams. Those of us blessed with the brains to understand leveraged effort have no excuse for unfulfilled dreams once we've selected a great company. That is, those of us who spend the majority of our time recruiting instead of procrastinating and babysitting the downline.

Affirmation

"I achieve great things because I focus on wealth through front-line recruiting."

Week Twenty Three

Fun and Work Do Mix

"If you aren't having fun, you're doing it wrong." Mark Yarnell

As I think back over my entire career in networking, there's one quality which seems to be evident among the most successful: they are having fun. In fact, some of them appear to be "slightly off," if you know what I mean. A little crazy perhaps. In the voices and answering machines of leaders, you often hear passion and humor.

Of course, most people think that big money earners are passionate because they're earning a million dollars a year. But I think it's the other way around. I've had countless calls from people who can't seem to recruit leaders off the Internet. One person said he sent out a ton of spams, yet only recruited 10 people, none of whom went to work.

I suggest that there's no such thing as virtual passion. MLM has always been a relationship business in which people join us because they sense our joy and meaningful passion. It's not something that can be shared electronically.

Dare to be a little crazy. Don't worry about what others think; the greatest waste of time is Impression Management. Have fun over your telephone. Play with people, especially the professionals who may have not had a good day in 20 years (you can hear it in their adversarial voices).

Have fun, because in our industry if you aren't enjoying every day, you're doing something wrong.

Affirmation

"I thoroughly enjoy every aspect of Network Marketing and appreciate with an undercurrent of fun in my business."

Week Twenty Four

Accept Our Differences

"Let's stop forming our MLM wagon train in a circle and firing inward." Mark Yarnell

I couldn't make any sense out of the recent (September 11, 2001) terrorist acts until I began to observe the behavior of people in our own industry. Each of us has a different method of coping with tragedy. Immediately following the bombing, some people chose immobilization and news observation. Three days after the bombing, many individuals were still glued to newscasts of replays of the events of that Tuesday. Others went into extended periods of anxiety and depression. Some folks went back to work immediately and some even used the advantage of a home-based business as a selling point. What soon emerged was an unbelievable reaction to these different coping mechanisms: the same character defect that led to the tragedies: intolerance.

I began getting emails the following Friday from people who were livid about those who would dare to go back to recruiting. Others were upset that they couldn't pull their distributors away from CNN news. Some argued that praying or crying was useless while others were enraged that their associates had turned off the news. Regardless of the different responses, what amazed me was the lack of tolerance some MLMers had for their own associates. If people can become enraged at business partners because of the manner in which they express pain and grief, how much easier it becomes to understand why huge economic, political and religious gaps lead to rage and terrorism.

We may not be able to bridge the gaps in global cultural differences, but do you suppose we MLM leaders could maybe accept each other in spite of different companies, products and grief coping strategies? If people want to work, so be it. If people want to watch CNN, so be it. If people want to use the terrorism as a graphic example of the benefits of working at home, so be it.

Intolerance led to the problem in the first place. I suggest we stop wasting time criticizing others and start accepting our people's right to cope with life in their own manner!

Whenever a company gets into trouble with regulators, MLM becomes a feeding frenzy. When MLMers put up phoney web sites or lead others to derogatory ones about our industry leaders, everyone gossips about the lies. If we are to ever take our respected place among all other systems of capitalism, we're going to eventually have to stop forming our wagon train in a circle and firing inwards. If we can't even tolerate or value ourselves, how can we ever expect to be respected by others?

Affirmation

"I choose to accept that other people have their own ways of conducting themselves and to be responsible for my own behavior rather than criticize others."

Week Twenty Five

Live MLM With Honor

"Give me MLM or give me death!" Mark Yarnell

Recently, a financial planner asked me why in the world I choose to spend my most productive years in Network Marketing. My answer was swift and decisive: because Networking rewards productivity, leveraged productivity. I would be embarrassed to admit that I was in any profession that encourages security-based salaries. Companies can keep their salaries, pensions, health plans, and Fords. Give me an unlimited opportunity or give me death! I'd rather buy my own dream car than drive a free Taurus. I never wanted to be a doctor because I could only help one person at a time. I never wanted to be a lawyer because there are only a few billable hours every day.

No thanks, folks! I'm a network marketer and proud to admit it. In fact, I'd be embarrassed to be anything else. I'm in a pyramid where everyone starts at the top and fills in the bottom, instead of at the bottom and clawing toward some elusive top. I win when others win, not when they lose because I was promoted ahead of them. I give money to charities and I found them. I don't have any structured hours but I'm on the phone fifty or more hours a week because I love interacting with winners. I could take more vacations but I've had my fill of poverty and behind most beautiful beaches is a ghetto. I'm tired of watching beer-guzzling vacationeers beat down Mexicans to the last peso on shell jewelry and trinkets. Every day spent at home with people I love is heaven on earth.

So the next time some "Big Business" person questions MLM – don't hesitate to express pride in what you do. Networkers are champions in the last bastion of true capitalism!

Affirmation

"It's easy for me to contact people about my business because I'm proud and excited to be succeeding in this noble profession."

CHAPTER THIRTEEN

The Warrior's Creed

"Warriors choose to live adventurous lives
and, through their actions and deeds,
pass the ideals of this creed
on to future generations."

I WAS FORTUNATE TO GROW UP IN THE FARMLANDS of Missouri with a grandmother who was a full-blooded Cherokee Native. She died when I was quite young, but not before introducing me to one simple principle: the importance of a personal creed.

She said that among her people each group had its own particular creed and that warriors had the most provocative one of all. In 1986 when I was failing miserably at all my endeavors, I thought about my grandmother's idea and decided to write and follow my own warrior's creed.

After compiling it, I faxed it to three of my friends and actually heard nothing about it for several years. In 1990, I received a request from a major corporation to reprint the Warrior's Creed as a poster and send it to their executives as a Christmas gift. After getting it copyrighted, I gave others permission to reprint it and many people have done so over the years. I am astounded at the number of people who have adopted this creed as their own personal business doctrine. Several million dollar earners have posted it on their refrigerators and bathroom mirrors and made it a point to call me personally and express their appreciation.

This is the first time my creed has been printed and distributed commercially and I hope you'll find meaning in its words. Free enterprise has always seemed like a highly competitive battle to most folks but, armed with the "Warrior's Creed," one need never feel defeated. And to Nanny, wherever you are, thanks for giving me wings.

Warrior's Creed 1

WARRIORS REFUSE TO BE BRAINWASHED BY THE "SECURITY MYTH." THEIR LIVES ARE GIVEN MEANING BY THE ADVENTURE OF RISK AND UNCERTAINTY. THEY ALWAYS LIVE ON THE CUTTING EDGE, AWARE THAT SECURITY CAN NEVER EXIST IN A CONSTANTLY CHANGING WORLD.

Warrior's Creed 2

WARRIORS ARE ALWAYS POISED, AGILE AND CUNNING, SO THAT WHEN ANY WINDOW OF OPPORTUNITY IS OPENED EVEN SLIGHTLY, THEY CAN CLIMB THROUGH IT WITH SWIFTNESS AND PRECISION. RISK AND CHANGE ARE THEIR MOST EAGERLY ANTICIPATED OCCURRENCES.

Warrior's Creed 3

WARRIORS SEEK AND CHERISH THE COMPETITION OF OTHER WARRIORS, AWARE THAT TO COMPETE IS TO TEST, IMPROVE AND HONE THEIR SKILLS. THEY THRIVE ON COMPETITION.

Warrior's Creed 4

WARRIORS ANSWER TO NO ONE AND REFUSE TO GIVE EVEN
ONE HOUR OF CONTROL OF THEIR DESTINIES TO OTHERS,
FULLY AWARE THAT THEY HAVE THE WISDOM AND POWER
TO BEST SHAPE THEIR OWN LIVES.

Warrior's Creed 5

WHEN WARRIORS FIND OPPORTUNITIES TO SUCCEED THEY
PUT THEIR HANDS TO THE PLOW AND NEVER LOOK BACK.
PERSEVERANCE AND COMMITMENT ARE THE
CORNERSTONES OF THEIR SUCCESS.

Warrior's Creed 6

WARRIORS NEVER FEAR FAILURE, RIDICULE OR DEFEAT
BECAUSE ONLY QUITTERS AND WHINERS DETEST THESE
PERIODIC BUT INEVITABLE SETBACKS.

Warrior's Creed 7

WARRIORS ARE DISCOVERED BY THEIR ACTIONS, NOT THEIR WORDS. TO CLAIM THAT ONE IS A WARRIOR IS, IN ITSELF, A REFLECTION OF ARROGANT MEDIOCRITY.

Warrior's Creed 8

WARRIORS BELIEVE RULES ARE TO BE BROKEN AND AUTHORITY IS TO BE QUESTIONED. THEY REMAIN LOYAL ONLY TO IDEALS OF INTEGRITY AND HONESTY, FULLY AWARE OF THE DIFFERENCE BETWEEN RIGHT AND WRONG. IN THE LIFE OF THE WARRIOR THERE IS NO GRAY AREA, BECAUSE THEY RECOGNIZE THAT IF A PERSON WILL STEAL AN EGG, HE'LL STEAL AN OX.

Warrior's Creed 9

WARRIORS ARE DREAMERS WHO ALWAYS MAINTAIN ALTRUISTIC GOALS BIGGER THAN THEMSELVES. WHEN WARRIORS HAVE MATERIAL POSSESSIONS, SO DO THEIR FRIENDS AND FAMILIES, BECAUSE TO SHARE IS TO KNOW TRUE JOY.

Warrior's Creed 10

WARRIORS ASPIRE TO THE HIGHEST CALLING IN LIFE. THEY CHOOSE TO LIVE ADVENTUROUS LIVES WITH THE PRIMARY INTENT OF PASSING THE IDEALS OF THIS CREED ON TO FUTURE GENERATIONS VIA THEIR ACTIONS AND DEEDS.

Warrior's Creed 11

WARRIORS ARE ON A PERPETUAL QUEST FOR EXCELLENCE IN EVERYTHING THEY DO WHILE MANY POOR SOULS BECOME RELEGATED TO LIVES OF QUIET DESPERATION.

Warrior's Creed 12

GIVEN ALL THE FACTS, WARRIORS CAN MAKE RATIONAL DECISIONS IN ONE MINUTE. THEY DETEST ANALYSIS AND REFUSE TO WASTE TIME DABBLING IN MINUTIAE.

Warrior's Creed 13

THE PRIORITIES OF A WARRIOR ARE GOD, FAMILY, WISDOM AND SUCCESS. THE ORDER OF THOSE PRIORITIES IS SELDOM ALTERED EXCEPT BY OCCASIONAL ERRORS IN JUDGMENT, AND ONCE DISCOVERED THE WARRIOR QUICKLY ADJUSTS THE MISTAKE.

Warrior's Creed 14

WARRIORS ACCEPT ALL RESPONSIBILITY FOR THEIR OWN ACTIONS AND RECOGNIZE THAT LEADERSHIP IS A PROCESS OF DEMONSTRATING WHAT IS POSSIBLE.

Warrior's Creed 15

WARRIORS ARE NEVER CRYBABIES. THEY ADHERE RIGOROUSLY TO THE MOST STRINGENT STANDARDS OF LEADERSHIP, POWER AND SELF-CONTROL. TEMPORARY UNHAPPINESS IS QUICKLY REPLACED BY ENTHUSIASM.

Warrior's Creed 16

WARRIORS LOVE OTHERS ENOUGH TO ALWAYS TELL THEM
THE TRUTH EVEN IF PAINFUL, AND WELCOME THE TRUTH
FROM OTHERS WITHOUT CONSIDERING CRITICISM
A PERSONAL ATTACK.

Warrior's Creed 17

WARRIORS REMAIN CONSTANTLY ON FIRE WITH
ENTHUSIASM IN AN EFFORT TO ILLUMINATE THE PATHS OF
THOSE ASPIRING WARRIORS WHO COME FROM MILES
AROUND TO WATCH THEM BURN.

Warrior's Creed 18

ABOVE ALL ELSE, WARRIORS UNDERSTAND THAT THE SEED
OF A WARRIOR LIES DORMANT IN EVERY HUMAN SOUL. THE
ULTIMATE GOAL OF ALL WARRIORS IS TO REVEAL AND
NURTURE THOSE SEEDS FOR ALL WHO WILL LISTEN,
KNOWING THAT THEIR OWN PERSONAL WORTH WILL SOME
DAY BE MEASURED BY THE NUMBER OF WARRIORS
THEY LEFT BEHIND.

I AM OFTEN ASKED WHY I DECIDED TO DEDICATE MY ADULT LIFE to MLM. One corporate CEO recently asked me that question after retaining me as keynote speaker at his annual sales banquet. He pointed out that, with stock options, his earnings exceeded mine. When I asked him how much his best ten managers earned, he failed to see the purpose of my question. That's the primary difference between traditional companies and network marketing. In other professions, you start at the bottom of a pyramid and try to claw your way to the top spot by beating your associates. In MLM, you begin at the very top of your own structure and succeed by filling in the bottom as you elevate your associates.

Keep in mind at all times that MLM is an *acceptable, legitimate* business. I will go anywhere, any time to debate any human being about that. I have close friends who run companies, practice law and medicine, teach, sell computers and excel at public relations. But those jobs are just jobs. Everyone is out for themselves. In our profession, no one wins unless dozens of others win. Nobody gets to earn billions unless his or her managers get the same shot.

If you are considering our industry, pay close attention to one fact: if one person wins, it's because thousands have won. Age, color, sex, experience and scholastic degrees have no value unless you produce. That's what makes MLM great. We are a productivity-based industry in which common people can reach for the stars. MLM is the greatest industry in free enterprise. Period. End of story. And when anyone tries to persuade you otherwise, they are in bondage to ignorance. The only people who detest our industry are those who have failed because they didn't understand how to pick a great company, or those who would rather have a weekly paycheck than an unlimited opportunity. People fail; MLM doesn't.

Imagine the poor guy sitting on death row for a murder he didn't commit because he had a court appointed attorney who was incompetent. That guy will swear that the US legal system is a scam. A guy who does commit a murder and can afford great lawyers to select incompetent jurors, who return a verdict of innocent, will go to his grave swearing that our legal system works. Who's right? Neither. Any system can be prostituted by those who replace values with money as the only adult report card.

Look closely at human institutions and you'll discover that systems don't fail people; people fail systems. We can't throw out western civilization's system of laws because certain people place winning above being right. Just because one group of high-powered lawyers manipulates the system doesn't mean that all lawyers are valueless.

The fact that some people who start MLM companies and some field leaders have no values doesn't mean that MLM isn't a legitimate profession. Lack of values can make any profession seem absurd. I'm sure the U.S. President wants terrorists tried in military courts for fear that with the right lawyers they'll all be living in Florida playing golf and signing book deals a year after any trial, regardless of guilt or innocence. The fact that there are now more lawyers in one high rise building in Seattle than in the entire nation of Japan speaks volumes about what happens when people in any profession prioritize dollars ahead of values. But that's certain people, not the entire profession.

The biggest problem in MLM results from all the in-fighting. Whenever a company is in trouble, other distributors circle like sharks. We even have distributors who put up web sites pretending to be honest industry watchdogs, then denigrate their competitors. By contrast, lawyers and other professionals have learned the power of blaming everyone except themselves. During a recent airing of *American Justice* on A&E, people were lamenting the fact that a murderer was found innocent and because of double jeopardy, could not be tried again in spite of new evidence that proved his guilt. The only thing the defense attorneys, prosecutors and judge were in agreement about was that it was the jury's fault. In MLM, any time one company gets in trouble, we form our wagon train in a circle and fire inward. In other professions, they have learned to blame everyone else.

In MLM, success depends on effort, not celebrity or dream teams. I wrote this book to give everyone a level playing field. However, nothing you read will be of any value until you recognize a simple fact: MLM is a great profession that provides equal opportunity for each of us. To get to the big dollars, you can't be ashamed of your profession. So remember, our industry is the last bastion of legitimate free enterprise in which common people can rise to their full potential by distributing a legitimate product to end consumers through an international network of "word of mouth" marketing professionals. Self-reliance is the key. Competence is the cornerstone. I hope that this book has provided a little of both. The rest is up to you.

Oh, and one final thought: above all else remember this, we are a Performance-Based Industry as opposed to a Security-Based Profession. Nine out of ten people in America are limited by the security myth. Simply put, here we are hurtling through space at 63,000 mph on a piece of dust called earth toward "God only knows" what cosmic destination or far reaches of an infinite universe and some people are worried about their pensions. Get it?

The key to our industry consists in finding the one performance-based entrepreneur out of every ten prospects, not attempting to change and motivate the other nine. I was one of those rare guys who never raised my hand to ask permission to go to the bathroom. Even in the first grade I realized that Mrs. Knabb had no idea how full my bladder was. I got in some trouble, but I never cared because I was not about to turn control of my internal organs over to her. If I had to go, I went. The other kids raised their hands and crossed their legs. By adulthood, most folks are sheep and certainly not interested in performance-based industries. Give them a

Taurus, health insurance, a cubicle and mediocre pension and they're happy as a hog in slop. Best of all, they get to earn a weekly check by simply putting in time. Lawyers, doctors, executives and other professionals are 90 percent security-based folks.

Here's my advice... Find the one winner in ten and teach him or her everything you know. Don't try to convert frogs to eagles. Our education system churns out robots all day, every day who need structure and authority figures to succeed. You won't change that fact nor is it right to criticize security-based professionals for their choices. Find the 100,000 good performers in every one million and you've done your job. The greatest thing about our industry is that you only need to find about ten to wind up with thousands. How about them apples!

About the Author

Mark Yarnell has won numerous awards in Network Marketing and co-authored three bestsellers including *Your First Year in Network Marketing* and *Self-Wealth*. Besides earning a big pile of money, teaching the only college certificate course in Network Marketing, and serving as contributing editor to *Success* magazine for eight years, Yarnell is an avid paragliding and ultralite pilot. He and his wife, Valerie, and their children Amy, Christine and Eric live in different places, but keep their dogs Emily and Winnie at home in British Columbia, where they continue to build their Legacy for Life organization. Mark and Valerie are Independent Distributors with Legacy for Life.

Send any comments to: MarkYarnell@self-wealth.com

Index

R

recruiting 164

    six steps in 81

rejection 149

risk 139

S

scams 72-73

Schrieder, Tom 37

self-sabotage

    avoiding 151

self-worth 91

Soros, George 27

spouse

    asking for support from 122

    honesty with 120–121

    talking about failure with 122

    unsupportiveness of 119-123

Stone, W. Clement 65

straightforward selling 76

Success magazine 33-36

T

tabula rosa 43, 52

teamwork 162

tenacity 143

The Legend 34-36

Thomas, Dave 27

three-way call 81

tools

    making the greatest

      set of 58-59

    myth of Internet 73-74

    recruiting 45

triggering cues 44

Trump, Donald 21

Turner, Ted 27

W

warm market 45-51

    memory jogger 47-51

    tools 45

Wilkins, Curt 55

Williams, A.L. 64

To Order Books:

Visit Mark Yarnell online at:

www.self-wealth.com

Obtain Mark Yarnell's book and other product information:

(800) 460-8604

(product inquiries only, please)